This much needed addition to the literature is a must read for all who are struggling with depression.

> —Mira Kirshenbaum, author of *The Emotional Energy Factor* and *Everything Happens for a Reason*

If depression could talk, and if you could listen, it would jump up and down, saying, "I'm trying my best to tell you something. Please listen to me!" If you let this book show you how to listen, you and your world can be so much better! This is my gift to you!

> —Alvin R. Mahrer, Ph.D., professor emeritus of psychology at the University of Ottawa, Canada, and author of *The Complete Guide to Experiential Psychotherapy*

Is depression a gift? This book by Honos-Webb makes a strong and provocative case that despite its accompanying pain, depression provides an opportunity to take stock and start anew. Written with sensitivity and intelligence, The Gift of Depression is both important and accessible. It deserves the careful attention of all.

> —Christopher Peterson, Ph.D., professor of psychology at the University of Michigan, Ann Arbor, and author of *A Primer in Positive Psychology*

The Gift of Depression is one of those break-through books that can profoundly alter your view of yourself. If you have ever been depressed—or are even now feeling confused or uncertain about what to do next—this book has the potential to turn on the light of understanding—maybe even of inspiration!

> —Carol Adrienne, Ph.D., author of *The Purpose of Your Life*

listening
to
depression

How
Understanding Your Pain
Can Heal Your Life

LARA HONOS-WEBB, PH.D.

New Harbinger Publications, Inc.

Publisher's Note

This publication is designed to provide accurate and authoritative information in regard to the subject matter covered. It is sold with the understanding that the publisher is not engaged in rendering psychological, financial, legal, or other professional services. If expert assistance or counseling is needed, the services of a competent professional should be sought.

Disclaimer

Case studies have been fictionalized and names have been changed to various degrees, in order to protect the confidentiality of the individuals who inspired the stories in this book.

Distributed in Canada by Raincoast Books

Copyright © 2006 by Lara Honos-Webb
New Harbinger Publications, Inc.
5674 Shattuck Avenue
Oakland, CA 94609
www.newharbinger.com

Cover design by Amy Shoup; Cover image: Constantini Michele/PhotoAlto/Getty Images; Acquired by Melissa Kirk; Edited by Karen O'Donnell Stein; Text design by Tracy Marie Carlson

Library of Congress Cataloging-in-Publication Data

Honos-Webb, Lara.
   Listening to depression : how understanding your pain can heal your life / Lara Honos-Webb.
      p. cm.
   ISBN-13: 978-1-57224-443-6
   ISBN-10: 1-57224-443-7
   1. Depression, Mental—Popular works.   I. Title.
RC537.H66 2006
616.85'27—dc22

                                                     2006022228

08   07   06
10   9   8   7   6   5   4   3   2   1
First printing

This book is gratefully dedicated to Ken, Kenny and Audrey Webb for the cozy joy, love, and laughter they share with me.

Contents

Chapter 1

How Cutting Off Depression Makes It Worse

Depression is meant to stop you in your tracks. It is your signal that something is wrong and needs to be healed. The premise of this book is that the main symptoms of depression—insomnia or hypersomnia, fatigue and loss of energy, and feelings of worthlessness—are in the service of transforming your life. To some, the idea that depression can be viewed as a gift may be offensive. They may think such a view does not take into account the real suffering and pain of depression. It's true that there are times when depression is not a gift (see chapter 11), but in many cases it can be seen as a meaningful experience to be honored.

Because anyone going through a depression experiences pain and suffering, the following metaphors are provided for you to understand how your experience can be both painful and essentially meaningful at the same time. If depression is an attempt at self-healing, as I will propose, then cutting off depression can be harmful. In this chapter we will review some metaphors that may help you understand how depression can be a gift and recognize the complications that can result from trying to cut off depression.

SOME HELPFUL METAPHORS

One way of reconciling the pain of the depression with its potential for healing is to understand that pain is meant to get your attention. There is a Sufi story about a man who falls asleep under a tree. Another person sees a poisonous snake crawl into the sleeping man's mouth and runs over to the person and starts beating him up to get him to wake up and get the snake out. The pain of being beaten wakes up the sleeping man, who does not realize that the person beating him up is actually trying to save his life. Depression can be similar, in that it is trying to tell you to see that something is not working in your life. The following metaphors illustrate different aspects of this function of depression.

The Fly Banging Against a Window

I once noticed a fly inside a car banging its head repeatedly against a car window, trying to escape from the car. The irony was that the window on the other side of the car was open, and all it had to do was stop trying to move forward, turn around, and fly out the other side. Similarly, there are times when if you force yourself to try to move forward and overcome obstacles by sheer force of will you may cause yourself great injury, without success. There are times when the most effective strategy is to stop in your tracks and contemplate your situation rather than bulldozing ahead. For example, if the fly had stopped and turned around, it might have noticed the other window, which offered an easy escape into freedom.

Depression, which often leads to a withdrawal of life energy from current life situations, may be a gift that allows you to reorient yourself and find an alternative strategy for solving your life's problems. Unlike the fly, you can turn around and reevaluate your situation. For example, Lisa, who was married to a man addicted to gambling, spent much of her time taking responsibility for his actions, trying to get him to stop, and attempting to solve the problems he created. A clinical depression forced her to reevaluate her strategy for coping with her husband's gambling. She came to realize that her energies would better be spent investing in her own life. She considered a career change and other activities that nurtured herself. Her depression lifted as she channeled her energies into her own life, rather than into trying to change her husband (Honos-Webb et al. 2006; Honos-Webb et al. 2002; Honos-Webb et al. 1998).

Aviation Navigation

When a plane flies across the country it uses a navigation system to help it stay on its flight path so it will get where it is supposed to go and not interfere with other airplanes in flight. If the plane deviates even slightly from its trajectory, the navigation system alerts the pilot and the corrective changes are made so that the airplane stays on course. Similarly, depression can be a signal alerting you that you have veered off course and warning you to change your direction. For example, Jan found herself overwhelmed by the demands of her siblings, who expected her to take care of their parents and to be responsible for all family get-togethers (Honos-Webb et al. 1999). She also struggled to take care of her husband, who refused to take on any household responsibilities. Jan worked a full-time job in sales and her personal motto was "The customer always comes first."

She exhausted herself trying to control her husband and meet the expectations of her relatives. She found herself sinking into a depression. During therapy she learned that her depression was a signal that she had gotten off course by always putting others' needs ahead of her own and failing to take care of herself. In therapy, she learned to understand that depression was a signal telling her to respect herself. She learned to say no to the demands of her relatives. She learned to assert herself with her husband. In this way, she was able to transform her depression from a destructive symptom into a communication to take care of herself, to put herself first.

Pruning

Depression also may be a signal that you need to cut off a part of yourself in order to make room for something new to grow. You may need to cut off parts of yourself that have outlived their usefulness so that you can make new developmental leaps. Sarah grew up in a family where she learned that she could not trust anyone. When she was a child, this strategy protected her from being victimized. However, as an adult, when she found herself isolated, she struggled with a full-blown major depression (see "Major Depressive Disorder" later in this chapter).

Through the self-exploration prompted by her depression, Sarah realized that her difficulty trusting others no longer served her in her adult life, since she could now use her judgment to protect herself and to determine who was and was not trustworthy. By learning to cut back her distrust, she allowed her ability to connect with others to grow. In this way, her depression stopped her in her tracks, causing her to examine what wasn't working in her life. Through reevaluating her beliefs toward others she was able to change her foundational beliefs and move toward creating intimacy with others (Honos-Webb, Stiles, and Greenberg 2003).

The Hibernation

Everyone knows that bears hibernate in the winter to survive the harsh conditions and to conserve energy for the springtime. The slowing down and withdrawal of energy that occurs in a depression may also help you to get through a difficult life experience and to conserve energy during a life cycle change. Such a view is consistent with evolutionary theory, which explains the adaptive nature of withdrawal from an environment that is punishing. One evolutionary theory of depression, the behavioral shutdown model, suggests that it makes sense to retreat from any behavior that has high costs and little return, and instead consider a more worthwhile way of investing one's life energy (Henriques 2000).

Jim found himself struggling in his final year of college to meet the many demands of his advanced courses. He had struggled with a learning disorder much of his life and his final year was almost more than he could take. He found himself feeling depressed and withdrew from his many social activities and hobbies. Instead of going to the bar with his friends he stayed home and slept. Instead of going skiing over the holiday break he just stayed inside and rested.

He came to see that there had been wisdom in his withdrawal. He knew he needed to graduate in order to achieve his life goals, but because of his learning disorder he had very real challenges to overcome in his final year as classes became more rigorous. He realized that to survive the more rigorous conditions he would have to withdraw his energy from activities unrelated to his studies. He needed to devote all of his energy to his schoolwork. By spending his free time resting or sleeping, he was really conserving his energy in order to most effectively meet his scholarly challenges. He also came to understand that a college degree would allow him to pursue his dreams. And his dreams would not make the same demands on him as his college classes did. He realized that by saving his energies for his courses now, he would later be able to reinvest energy in his social life and other activities.

The River Lethe

In Greek mythology, it was believed that after death people had to drink from the river Lethe in Hades in order to forget their life on earth. To many people, depression may feel like a mini death as they lose interest in their daily activities and begin thinking that their life may be meaningless. Similarly, depression may help you to disconnect from a previous lifestyle or situation so that you can create a new life. It may be that there is wisdom in finding your old life to be pointless. Jack, for example, was married at a young age to a beautiful woman but found himself divorced a few years later. He lost interest in all his old social ties, while he struggled with depression. It seemed that all his previous friends were connected with his ex-wife, who traveled in impressive social circles. He began to experience their status as meaningless as he turned down invitations and withdrew from everyone connected to his previous life. While he struggled with his feelings of emptiness, he realized that he had never enjoyed these social connections. Instead, he was much more interested in some of his new friends, who were more bohemian and less impressed with social status and accomplishments. He came to understand that both his choice of marriage partner and their circle of friends were out of alignment for him in view of his true interests and values, which steered him toward friends and partners who were creative and authentic and shared his offbeat view of life. Because of his depression, he fully disconnected from his previous life, allowing him to find his deepest values and interests and pursue a life in line with those.

WHAT IS DEPRESSION?

Many people will describe themselves as being depressed at some time in their life. The word "depression" is often used in place of "disappointed" or "sad." You might say you are depressed because you didn't get the job you wanted, or because your latest romantic relationship did not work out. In the field of psychology, depression refers to a spectrum of mood disorders that result in clinical impairment and reduced level of functioning.

What this means is that not only do you feel bad but you also can't do what you used to be able to do. In short, it seems like you are broken or have fallen apart. Someone who experiences clinical symptoms of depression may be diagnosed with a major depressive disorder, a dysthymic disorder, bipolar disorder, or cyclothymia, all of which are separate diagnoses. Bipolar disorder involves depression alternating with manic episodes, which are periods when a person feels elated and has an enormous amount of energy that may get him or her into trouble. Cyclothymia indicates a chronic alternation between low-grade depression and low-grade mania. This book will focus on major depressive disorder and dysthymia, which is a diagnosis in its own right indicating a low-grade, unremitting depression. While some of the concepts in this book may be relevant for someone with a bipolar or cyclothymia diagnosis, in general these more complex mood disorders are more likely to be biologically based and require medical management.

Major Depressive Disorder

The lifetime risk for a major depressive disorder ranges from 10 to 25 percent for women and from 5 to 12 percent for men (American Psychiatric Association 2000). The higher rates in women have been attributed to multiple causes, including societal discrimination;

hormonal differences; the physiological and psychological demands of pregnancy, childbirth, and mothering; and the multiple expectations women face in their professional and family roles.

Estimates indicate that in 1999 approximately 27 million people suffered from a depressive disorder in the United States and an additional 29 million suffered from depressive symptoms (Henriques 2000). The annual costs associated with major depression in the United States are an estimated $44 to $55 billion (Lerner et al. 2004), comparable to costs associated with coronary heart disease (Hirschfeld et al. 1997). It is expected that depression will become the second leading cause of disability worldwide in the next decade and that by 2010 it will be the most costly of all illnesses (Collins et al. 2004). Media outlets report increasing rates of depression in adolescents, as reported in *Newsweek* (Wingert and Kantrowitz 2002). Estimates suggest that as many as 25 percent of adolescents experience at least one depressive episode before the age of eighteen (Lewinsohn et al. 1993). Up to 15 percent of individuals with severe major depression die by suicide.

The main requirement for a diagnosis of major depressive disorder is either a depressed mood experienced most of the time for at least two weeks or a dramatic loss of interest in almost all customary activities. In addition to these symptoms, a person must report four of the following symptoms:

■ Unexplained or unusual weight loss or weight gain

■ Insomnia or hypersomnia

■ Physical slowing down or physical agitation

■ Fatigue and loss of energy every day

■ Feelings of worthlessness and inappropriate guilt

■ Difficulty concentrating

■ Recurrent thoughts of death or suicide

As you can see from this list of symptoms, depression affects not only the level of emotional distress but also bodily functioning, so sleeping, eating, and physiological activity are changed by the experience of a depression. Depression profoundly alters both the body and the mind.

It can be difficult for you to determine if you are clinically depressed without consulting a trained psychiatrist or psychologist. Sometimes people think they are clinically depressed when they are simply experiencing a reasonable reaction to a difficult life circumstance. Someone who has gone through a recent loss is likely to be experiencing grief, which can be confused with depression. Grief and pain are part of every human life, but they don't necessarily indicate or lead to the clinical disorder of depression.

In contrast, some people may have been depressed for quite some time but not recognize it in themselves. These people may think they have to tough it out and try to bulldoze through each day without giving themselves the special attention they need—attention that would allow them to realize that their lives don't have to be this way. Sometimes people don't recognize they're depressed because they know that their problems aren't as bad as those of others, and so they tell themselves that they shouldn't and can't be depressed. This logic is very deceptive because depression can strike anyone, no matter what their financial or social situation is. Some people don't recognize their depression, because they mask it by eating too much, working too hard, drinking too much, or using drugs. When people dull their pain with these behaviors, they typically create two problems instead of just one: depression and obesity, depression and a drug problem, or depression and workaholism.

So how do you find out whether you are depressed? Seek a professional consultation. This is especially important to do, because the condition can make it hard to see your life objectively. One of the most difficult conditions to self-diagnose is dysthymia.

Dysthymia

Dysthymia is a clinical disorder that shares many of the symptoms of depression. However, it causes less impairment in daily functioning and runs a chronic course, meaning that in order to warrant a diagnosis of dysthymia the person's symptoms must have lasted for at least two years and seem to be unremitting. In addition to having a depressed mood for more than two years, someone with dysthymia has two or more of the following:

■ Poor appetite or overeating

- Insomnia or hypersomnia

- Low energy or fatigue

- Low self-esteem

- Poor concentration or difficulty making decisions

- Feelings of hopelessness

As previously stated, the symptoms of dysthymia can overlap substantially with those of depression but are lower in intensity and last much longer. A major depressive disorder usually improves in four to six months, whereas dysthymia can be lifelong. Approximately 6 percent of the U.S. population will experience dysthymia during the course of their life (American Psychiatric Association 2000).

One reason that dysthymia may be difficult to recognize in oneself is that it becomes such a deep-rooted way of viewing one's self, world, and expectations for the future that it appears to be an accurate reflection of reality rather than a distortion caused by a psychological problem. Some psychologists have argued that dysthymia should be considered a personality disorder, because it is so pervasive in the person's way of being in the world. People suffering from dysthymia may become resigned to the fact that their worldview and chronic low-grade suffering are all they can expect from life. Occasionally, someone who suffers from dysthymia will also experience an episode of major depressive disorder, suffering from both illnesses at the same time.

The number of these full-blown disorders must be small in comparison to the number of people who experience lower-grade chronic levels of depression—people who do not meet the criteria for a clinical diagnosis of major depression or dysthymia but who experience feelings such as discouragement, despair, disapproval of the self, or a chronic disappointment with life itself. Although it is important, for treatment reasons, to make a distinction between clinical depressive disorders (major depression and dysthymia) and these other depressive symptoms, even low-level symptoms of depression can be helped by understanding the meaningfulness of these individual symptoms. In addition, it can be very important to face symptoms of depression even if they are not severe enough for a diagnosis, because a major depression is often preceded by lower-grade symptoms (Coyne, Pepper, and Flynn 1999).

Although most of this book is intended to help you discover how such symptoms can be seen as communications to you about your life course, the remainder of this chapter will focus on how the avoidance or masking of depressive symptoms can cause more problems than the depression itself.

HOW CUTTING OFF DEPRESSION MAKES MATTERS WORSE

Because of the psychological pain of depression, many people try to pretend it is not there or actively try to cut it off by choosing behaviors that numb the feelings. Frequently, these strategies actually intensify the depression and increase the complexity of the problems that may contribute to the depression. By facing depression directly, you can keep your depression from ballooning into such an unmanageable state that you cannot see the gifts that can be found in it.

Masked Depressions

Many psychologists use the term "masked depression" to mean the experience of a person who is depressed but does not directly report the symptoms of depression, because she has found a strategy to cover over or mask those symptoms. In many ways, a masked depression is more difficult to treat, because once the strategies for masking depression are removed the person is left to face the pain of depression. Therefore, this therapeutic work of "unmasking" depression can be felt as punishment, since the result of the therapy is the full experience of depression.

A Gift of Depression: Courage

Some of the main strategies people use to mask depression include overeating, drug and/or alcohol abuse, and compulsive overactivity, which lead to chronic fatigue. Because of the complexities that result from a life of masked depression, one gift of an unmasked depression is the capacity to face and feel the depression itself. This requires a great deal of courage and the ability to see life clearly. In this way, people who know they are depressed are at least one step ahead of people who suffer from masked depression. By staying in touch with your pain and the reality of your depression, you are much closer to finding the meaning and the message of your depression. The more effectively masked a depression is, the more difficult and lengthy the process of healing will be.

If you are in the middle of an agonizing depression, there is great hope for you. The more in touch you are with your pain, the closer you are to healing that pain. One psychological truism holds that "the only way out is through." To heal from your depression you must go all the way through it, and the more pain you are in, the more likely you are almost finished with the depression. The ways that people mask depression are discussed below, in addition to how these ways complicate healing from depression.

COMPULSIVE OVERACTIVITY: A LIFE OF TRIVIAL PURSUITS

One common and often-overlooked method for masking a depression is to keep so busy that you never have time to feel or to connect with your own experience. The pain of depression can drive you to avoid any internal reflection or connection to your emotional life. By compulsively keeping busy, you can block your painful emotions and troubling thoughts.

Because compulsive overactivity can look like the opposite of depression, it may be nearly impossible for others to detect the undercurrent of sadness. One of the giveaways is the compulsive nature of the activity. A common scenario is the workaholic who has difficulty coping when her compulsive outlet is taken away; to avoid this uncomfortable feeling, she makes sure every employee and customer stays connected to her by cell phone, fax, and e-mail while she is "vacationing" in Hawaii. Family members may complain that she almost panics at the thought of not being connected to her work life. For a woman with masked depression, inactivity means that she will have to face her internal demons, and so she does everything possible to avoid this.

Another characteristic of overactivity that masks depression is the triviality of the activities. This can be seen in the depressed woman who spends her time and money in a flurry of activity, shopping compulsively for the perfect shoes to match the perfect belt to match the perfect purse. Coordinating accessories is not a sign of depression in itself, but if the shopping is compulsive and chronic, and if the shopper feels an edge of uneasiness if she is not so occupied, then it may be a signal of an underlying depression.

Because overactivity is so highly valued in our culture, it is often rewarded. The rewards of workaholism are obvious. The more you work, the more income you may earn or the more praise you may receive. The more rewards you accumulate from compulsive overactivity, the more difficult it becomes for you to make any contact with your underlying depression, and the farther you get from your real values and interests. People who have a masked depression often have only superficial relationships and no real intimacy in their lives.

Unfortunately, the mask covering the depression is also brittle. At the first sign of cracking, the person's whole psychological structure is at risk of collapsing. For example, a person who masks a depression by working too much may be thrown into a profound depression or have suicidal impulses when she has a professional failure. Those feelings were there all the time, lurking beneath the brittle surface. By facing those hidden feelings directly you begin to gain control of your life rather than being driven by a desperate need to hide them.

OVEREATING

Overeating is a quick and easy way to dull or numb painful feelings. Overeating can also give you energy that seems to hide the despair and fatigue of depression. If you overeat to mask depression, it may take on such a habitual quality that at the first sign of a feeling of hopelessness or sadness you automatically reach for sweets or high-fat foods to dull the sense of emptiness and pain. In this way, you may never really recognize the underlying depression. You may struggle with your compulsive eating, but you may be unaware of the harshness of your emotional landscape.

Overeating complicates the underlying depression by preventing you from accessing depressed feelings and coping directly with them. Additionally, if you eat to mask depression you may wind up with a weight problem on top of your depression. Because of the harsh and exacting "thin ideal" for women in American culture, a weight problem can become a significant source of distress and low self-esteem in itself.

The reason the compulsive overeating maintains itself is that once you restrict your eating you come face to face with the depressive feelings, which feels like a punishment. Any behavior that increases pain is likely to be stopped pretty quickly. The only escape from this vicious circle is to practice increasing your tolerance of the pain that drives you to overeat.

The other problem with overeating is that it can intensify the underlying depression by increasing the feelings of worthlessness and the self-punishment that keep a depression going. A woman who eats too much often berates herself for not being in control of her eating. The more women beat up on themselves for their "bad behavior," the more they create an internal dialogue that they seek to avoid—by eating more. In this way, an underlying depression can be covered over by an increasingly toxic relationship to the self. This situation creates layers and layers of depression, which can obscure the underlying, possibly meaningful, depression, which may in fact contain a "gift" (a concept that will be discussed in the rest of the book).

DRUG AND ALCOHOL ABUSE

Someone with an underlying depression is more likely to become dependent on drugs or alcohol because the drug use is so rewarding. One widely held theory of human and even animal behavior holds that behaviors that are rewarded will increase and behaviors that are punished will decrease. In accordance with this universal theory, someone who is depressed and uses drugs is likely to find the behavior very rewarding and therefore use is likely to turn into abuse. Additionally, once a person stops using the drugs that are medicating the symptom of depression, the symptom is likely to return—along with symptoms of withdrawal. In this way, stopping use of the drug will seem very punishing, and this, too, will maintain the habit.

As a result, using drugs and/or alcohol to numb out a depression is probably the most insidious way of masking depression. And, to make matters worse, the complications of an addiction on top of a depression make it very difficult to access the underlying meaning of the depression. The reason for this is that addiction requires a great deal of work and commitment to recover from in itself, which is magnified when a depression lies underneath the addiction. Almost all the symptoms of depression can be medicated with drugs and/or alcohol.

Fatigue can be treated even by something as seemingly innocuous as caffeine.

More threatening to a person's life functioning is the use of cocaine or other stimulants. These drugs are more addictive and lead to serious impairments in health, relationships, and professional activities. Stimulants not only medicate fatigue but also temporarily boost self-esteem by providing a sense of grandiosity and an expanded feeling of self-confidence. Stimulants also can increase depressed people's ability to concentrate, allowing them to continue to function through a depression. Nicotine has psychological effects that are similar to those of stimulants. Cigarettes are actually the most dangerous of all depression-masking drugs, because they are the most common and can also be lethal. There is a large occurrence of cigarette smoking in depression; 70 percent of men and 80 percent of women with a history of major depression are estimated to have a smoking habit (Glassman et al. 1990).

Although alcohol is a depressant, it is often used to self-medicate depression because it is also disinhibiting. It may temporarily free you from the agitation of depression, the relentless pain and self-criticism. Alcohol is often used in an attempt to self-medicate insomnia. It may also serve as something like a general anesthetic in that it can simply numb you to your feelings and thoughts.

The complex dynamics of addiction illustrate the fundamental gift of depression. You can never run away from your legitimate pain; the effort to numb yourself from depression will lead to more pain. Your depression has meaning for you. You must stop and look at your depression directly. This book will help you find the meaning in your depression.

HOW FINDING THE GIFTS OF DEPRESSION WILL HELP YOU

Research has shown that the ability to make meaning of difficult life situations increases psychological and physical health (Taylor et al. 2000). This book will act as a guide for translating your symptoms of depression into meaningful communications to you about your life path. As the five metaphors at the beginning of the chapter (the fly banging against a window, aviation, pruning, hibernation, and the river Lethe) suggest, depression is a signal to stop and reevaluate what you are doing in your life and why.

Finding the gifts in your depression can be a strategy for healing yourself of depression. Albert Ellis, psychologist and founder of rational emotive behavior therapy, articulates how your beliefs about any "adversary" create emotions and behaviors that directly follow from those beliefs (2001). If depression is an adversary, the more you can take on beliefs about depression that will generate hope, the more you will be on your way to recovering from your depression.

Even if the gifts of depression are just illusions, your belief in the value of your depression will be healing in itself. Positive beliefs, even if they are inconsistent with objective facts, have been shown to improve mental health and produce measurable health benefits. Scientists found, in looking at AIDS and breast cancer, that "even unrealistic optimistic beliefs about the future may be health protective. The ability to find meaning in the experience is also associated with a less rapid course of illness. Taken together, the research suggests that psychological beliefs such as meaning, control, and optimism act as resources, which may not only preserve mental health in the context of traumatic or life-threatening events but be protective of physical health as well" (Taylor et al. 2000, p. 99).

Additionally, research has found that looking for and finding benefits in a difficult situation has positive outcomes in the form of improved mental health, and even extended survival following a heart attack or AIDS diagnosis (Tennen and Affleck 2002; Affleck et al. 1987). The positive effects of finding benefits even extend to victims of fire, disaster victims, mothers of acutely ill newborns, and those suffering from chronic pain. Real-world outcomes such as increased number of active days for arthritis sufferers result when individuals can find and remind themselves of the benefits of otherwise intensely negative experiences (Tennen and Affleck 2002).

Emerging research shows that hope is a robust and consistent predictor of life satisfaction (Isaacowitz, Vaillant, and Seligman 2003; Park, Peterson, and Seligman 2004). A large body of accumulating research consistently indicates that being able to make meaning of difficult life events is psychologically adaptive (Tedeschi, Park, and Calhoun 1998; Taylor et al. 2000). Therefore, the ability to make meaning out of stressful events could serve to protect you from increasing the severity of your depression. Making meaning of your depression itself might help you recover from the depression more quickly.

To put it simply, having a positive explanation for your depression will heal your depression. When something bad happens to you, how you explain it will affect the course of your depression and your health. A pessimistic explanatory style is one that views negative events as having internal causes, affecting all areas of your life, and being permanent. If you think depression is a brain disorder that is internally caused, affects all areas of functioning, and is likely to be permanent, then you have adopted a pessimistic explanation of your depression. Research has shown that the pessimistic explanatory style actually leads to more frequent and more severe depression, in addition to physical health problems including reduced immunity and complications for cardiac patients (Peterson, Seligman, and Vaillant 1988; Lin and Peterson 1990).

In contrast, the search for the gifts in depression allows for external explanation of the depression. This book will advance the argument that depression is a temporary reaction to the fact that the events of your life have gone off course.

The belief in your ability to have some control over stressful events will likely have positive effects on the depression itself (Chou and Chi 2001; Clark 2002). It has also been found that viewing change or a stressful event as a positive challenge reduces depression. The concept of "hardiness," the capacity to maintain a sense of control while looking for the positive in significant stressors, has been correlated with reduced illness, better psychological adjustment, and higher quality of life in addition to protection from depression (Clark 2002). If you believe you can find the gifts in your depression and have some measure of control over your symptoms, you have more power to recover rapidly.

The power of your psychological reaction to your depression is evident in the latest research on the efficacy of the placebo in treating depression. Researchers demonstrated that actual changes in the brain were found to correspond to the placebo effect in depression (Leuchter et al. 2002). Thus, hope and expectations can change your brain.

Because I really believe that depression can be a gift, I offer you these scientific findings to encourage you in the face of your doubt. Your skepticism and doubt about the gift of depression is predictable—in fact, it is a symptom of depression. A central feature of depression is a pessimistic viewpoint and low expectations for the self, the world, and the future. So if you find yourself doubting that there can be any value in mining your depression to find its gifts, you might want to consider that your doubt may be a symptom of your depression in itself. Do the following exercise if you find yourself feeling hopeless about trying to apply the healing program in this book.

First, you will want to get yourself a journal, which you can use throughout this book to record your responses to questions in the exercises. It will also allow you to reflect deeply on your experiences with the suggested activities. You can record your responses to the following exercise in the journal.

EXERCISE: DOUBT YOUR DOUBT

In this exercise you are asked to turn your symptoms of depression on their heads. This is one example of how depressive symptoms can be turned into gifts.

1. Write down any doubts you have about the gifts of depression. For example, you might find yourself saying:

    ■ Depression is not a gift. This is Pollyannaish.

    ■ I can't follow through on these exercises.

    ■ It's too hard to get a journal. I'll just skim through the exercises.

    ■ This will never work. I'm not going to waste my time.

2. Now write down pessimistic responses to your pessimistic thoughts. In short, doubt your doubts. Keep in mind that the doubting of your doubts will actually offer you a positive thought. If your negative thoughts are wrong, then something positive might result. This is similar to the truism that if a fool persists in her folly she will become wise. Examples might be the following:

    ■ What if I'm wrong? Depression might be a gift.

    ■ What if I were wrong about my efforts? What if I could do the exercises?

- I might be able to get a journal and take the exercises seriously.

- If these exercises do work, I might benefit.

3. Write down all your limits. What is stopping you from healing from depression? Here are some examples:

- I'm too tired to try to get better.

- My problems are too big.

- I'm not smart enough to solve my problems.

- I don't have enough money to get the help I really need.

4. Now write down serious doubts about the limits you have imposed on yourself. How might you be wrong about your own limits? Below are a few examples:

- Maybe I do have energy sometimes.

- Maybe I could solve some of my problems.

- What if I did have some answers to my problems? What would they be?

- Maybe I can get help without a lot of money. I don't know for sure.

After doing this exercise, reflect on this: if you think you are always wrong, then even your serious doubts may not be correct—and you may have more resources, skills, and hope than you imagine. By turning your doubt on itself, you open up the possibility that maybe you really are wrong about the hopelessness of your situation.

Doing this exercise prepares you for the next chapter, which suggests that each symptom of depression is a stage in a journey toward personal transformation. You may find this theory hard to believe. Just remember to keep doubting your doubts if you are tempted to dismiss the idea that there might be meaning in your suffering.

Chapter 2

The Gifts of Depression as Stages of a Journey

As we discussed in chapter 1, the fundamental gift of depression is that it is a wake-up call to make changes in your life. It is a call to stop and figure out what's wrong and do some problem solving. In this chapter, we will lay the foundation for the rest of the book, in which the symptoms of depression will be considered each in turn and the gifts of specific symptoms will be considered. This chapter briefly introduces you to each of the symptoms but suggests that you can look at the symptoms sequentially to view them as a journey of self-transformation.

By considering each symptom in turn, we learn something important: even if you do not meet the criteria for a diagnosis of depression (i.e., you have some symptoms but not all of those required for a diagnosis, a condition known as "sub-syndromal depression"), this book can still be useful to you. Someone with sub-syndromal depression could benefit by doing the exercises in this book and taking to heart the fundamental view that depression is meaningful. It might be that by hearing the message in the first symptoms of depression you could effect changes and prevent a full-blown depression from occurring.

So if you find yourself wondering whether you really are suffering from depression, but you do identify with some of the symptoms, keep reading. The symptoms of depression are meant to communicate important information to you, so the more skilled you become at hearing the message, the less troubled you'll be by depressive symptoms. It makes sense that if you can't hear someone whispering to you, then that person will eventually have to raise his voice or shout at you to get your attention. Similarly, the longer the symptoms go unheard, the louder, noisier, and more disruptive they will become.

CHANGE IN WORLDVIEW

The perspective suggested in this book does not offer just another technique for managing the symptoms of depression. Rather, it offers a fundamental change in worldview. Depression is not just a meaningless affliction to be eliminated—it is a communication to the self, from the self, about the self (Leitner, Faidley, and Celentana 2000). This view is at odds with the current understandings of depression and most forms of treatment (Honos-Webb 2005b; Honos-Webb and Leitner 2002; Honos-Webb and Leitner 2001). The dominant approach to treating depression is the medical model and its attendant treatment of choice—antidepressant medications.

Most depressed people who go to the doctor for treatment receive prescriptions for medicine alone rather than a recommendation for psychotherapy interventions, which have been shown to be equally effective. In one study, 88 percent of patients reporting depression received a treatment recommendation for antidepressant medication, while just 39 percent received a recommendation for psychotherapy (Collins et al. 2004). This practice goes against the existing scientific evidence that shows psychotherapy is an effective treatment for depression and that it has many benefits over medication. Some of the problems with medications include the following:

■   Improvements from medications are not maintained after the medication is stopped.

■ Some medications have more undesirable side effects, such as loss of sexual desire.

■ Clients are more likely to stop taking medication because of side effects. (Collins et al. 2004)

Some of the benefits of psychotherapy over medications include the following:

■ Psychotherapy is better tolerated, so clients are less likely to drop out.

■ Clients are less likely to refuse psychotherapy as a treatment option.

■ Psychotherapy can prevent relapse of depression more effectively than medications can.

■ Psychotherapy can be more cost effective, since medications need to be maintained long term, and psychotherapy may be helpful long after it is concluded. (Collins et al. 2004)

These data indicate that while individuals diagnosed with depression are most likely to receive medication, psychotherapy has proven to be equally effective and to have many benefits over antidepressant medication. Recent advances have shown that psychotherapy over the phone is an effective treatment for depression (Mohr et al. 2005). Telephone therapy substantially increases the adherence, while some studies have shown that as many as 33 percent of individuals who are given the medications just stop taking them (Jacobson and Hollon 1996) because of side effects. Among those who do adhere to medications, only 70 percent are helped (Holden 2003).

The approach used in this book is different even from that taken in most forms of psychotherapy that do not involve antidepressant medications. Most of these adopt the perspective that depression is a clinical disorder to be eliminated without considering the meaning or context of the symptoms. Therapy is usually focused on clarifying the client's impairments and working toward eliminating them. These approaches therefore keep the focus on clients' impairment rather than their strengths.

The practice of strength-based assessment encourages clinicians to pay attention to the strengths of the clients in addition to their impairments and disorders. While there is a growing recognition of the importance of strength-based assessment in the field of psychotherapy, "very little has been written offering guidance and ideas to clinicians about how to comment on client strengths in such a way as to promote therapeutic progress" (Gelso and Woodhouse 2003, p. 182). Therefore, if you go to a psychologist for help, you can predict that some of the feedback you will receive on what is wrong with you will be related to what psychologists are trained to do.

As important as strength-based assessment is, there is still a difference between the approach advocated in this book and the theory of strength-based assessment, which doesn't challenge the existence of an impairment. Rather, strength-based assessment looks for strengths alongside the diagnosis or impairment. Though it is important to actively look for a person's strengths in addition to depression, it is just as vital to see that there may be a gift, or message, in the depression itself.

The perspective proposed in this book may be at odds with the medical model, but it does not imply that depression should never be treated with medications. Many times, depression really does need to be managed with medications. See chapter 11 for techniques for reducing depressive symptoms and a discussion of how medications can be an important part of the journey toward transformation.

EXERCISE: STRENGTH-BASED ASSESSMENT

Now, take out your journal, reflect on the questions below, and write down your responses. The exercise will guide you through a strength-based assessment.

1. You are likely reading this book because you are depressed. One of the symptoms of depression is that it keeps you focused on the bad things in your life and it often prevents you from seeing the positive things in your life. You may be depressed, but that is not all that you are. In your journal, explore the following questions:

    ■   What else are you?

    ■   What strengths do you have that the depression has not overshadowed?

For example, you might write, "I am depressed, but I am also a mother" or "I am a professional." In reflecting on your strengths, you might write, "I am still a wonderful cook," or "I have overcome many difficulties in my life and therefore am strong and courageous."

2. After completing step 1, at the top of an empty journal page write the following heading: "Resources for Coping with Depression." Sometimes it can be helpful to simply accept the reality of your depression. As we discussed in chapter 1, the strategies people use to self-medicate or deny a depression often cause more problems, complicating the existing depression. To help you stay aware of your choices and supports that can keep you from self-medicating or denying your depression, you might want to complete the following sentence stems to guide your reflections:

- ■ "I am depressed, but one resource for helping me through the depression is _____ ." (List as many resources as possible.)

- ■ "I am depressed, but I can reach out for help. The following people can support me through this depression: _____ ." (List as many people as possible.)

- ■ "I am depressed, but one quality about myself that will help me through this depression is: _____ ." (List as many qualities as possible.)

- ■ "Even though I am depressed, I will not fall back on the self-destructive habit of _____ to cope with this depression."

- ■ "I am depressed, but there are many professionals who are trained to help people who are struggling like I am. The following professionals can guide me through this difficult time: _____ ." (List as many professionals as possible, such as a psychotherapist, a psychiatrist, a primary care doctor, an energy healer, a naturopath, or other provider.)

- "The family members who will be the most useful in helping me cope with depression are: _____ ."

- "The family members who will be least helpful during my depression are _____ , and I may consider setting strong boundaries with these people until I recover from this depression."

- "The things I can do that will help me cope with this depression are _____ ." (List as many activities as possible.)

3. After completing these sentences you can also write free-form reflections on resources available to help you cope with your depression.

A Gift of Depression: Emotional Sensitivity

After completing the above exercise, you can go a step further in looking for your strengths. In addition to looking for resources you have, you can start learning to reinterpret as a gift what may appear to be a deficit. This means that the problems you have, if looked at in a different way, can be seen as positive traits. Maybe you are more sensitive to other people and your emotional pain has to do with this level of connecting to other people. The very trait of your sensitivity can be a gift to others, who may benefit from your empathy. In his book *Care of the Soul*, author and psychologist Thomas Moore (1992, p. 144) writes that empathetic people "may have difficulty moving far enough away from emotional involvement to see what is going on, and to relate their life experiences to their ideas and values." Or, maybe your dark moods are related to your penetrating intelligence, which allows you to see realities that other people gloss over. If it is true that ignorance is bliss, then perhaps your intelligence leads to painful feelings that reflect the unpleasant realities that you see so clearly. There are many ways of finding the gifts in qualities that get labeled as depression.

EXERCISE: THE GIFTS OF DEPRESSION

This exercise will guide you through the process of developing your own ideas about the gifts your depression may offer. This is different from strength-based assessment in that you are not just listing resources for coping with depression—you are trying to creatively think of ways in which depression in itself, even its pain, its impairment in functioning, might have some meaning. Throughout this book I offer specific ways depression can be a meaningful experience, but you will likely find it helpful to generate your own ideas. There will be many gifts that are unique to your life that are not covered in this book.

1. Take out your journal and write "The Gifts of Depression" at the top of a blank page. Give yourself a half hour to reflect and write about how your depression could be a gift, or how it could be meaningful in your life. For example, Marianne wrote that her depression made her drop out of business school, and that the only classes she could take were the ones that seemed easy to her—courses in child development. She gravitated toward these classes because she loved children so much. She came to realize that if she had not gotten depressed she might have pressed on in business school, which would have set her up for a career she was not interested in. With her child-development background, however, she was able to work with children who had developmental delays and became a wonderful mother and a resource for her friends.

2. After writing your thoughts in response to item 1, consider the following sentence stems and write responses:

   - "I don't like this depression, but if it were serving a purpose in my life it might be _____ ."

   - "If it were not for this depression, one thing about my life that would be different is _____ ."

   - "My fatigue prevents me from doing _____ ."

   - "If I gave myself permission not to do these things, my life would _____ ."

- "Although I hate to admit it, one good thing about my depression is _____ ."

- "This depression has forced me to _____ ."

3. Finally, try the following thought experiment: Imagine that you wake up tomorrow morning and your depression is completely gone. You are relieved and amazed. However, there is one thing that concerns or confuses you about the rapid disappearance of your depression. What is it? Write the answer to this question in your journal. For example, Scott realized that if he completely lost his depression he might lose his emotional sensitivity, which allowed him to reach out to other people who were depressed but were not able to admit it to themselves or others. He realized he had a gift for feeling the pain of other people and could use this to connect with others on a deeper level than he might have if he had not become depressed. He was able to use this insight to think about ways he could preserve his sensitivity without the experience of a full-blown clinical depression.

DEPRESSION AS A JOURNEY TOWARD SELF-TRANSFORMATION

In the first chapter we discussed five metaphors for understanding the gifts of depression: the fly banging against a window, aviation, pruning, hibernation, and the river Lethe. Each of these metaphors points to the fact that an impairment in current functioning could actually provide you with a "time-out," an opportunity to reenvision and refigure one's life. The clinical model of treating depression assumes that the premorbid level of functioning (prior to the onset of the depression) generally represents a gold standard of sorts and that the goal of therapy is to return the person to the previous level of functioning.

However, your depression may be helping you to realize that in some way your prior level of "high" functioning was off track. One reason for depression may be to help you redefine your understanding of what is and is not high functioning.

The medical model of functioning does not take into account that development and growth often require a time of disequilibrium or breakdown. In order for things in your life to change, they need to be broken down so that you can reorganize and take in something new. For example, Lisa experienced her clinical depression as a breakdown, but upon reflection she realized that her belief that "you must always forgive" was too simple an approach to dealing with the complexities of life (Honos-Webb et al. 1998). Over the course of therapy she realized that she was allowed to be angry with people and that this anger helped her to set healthy limits with these people. In this way, her depression awakened her capacity to connect to others in ways that allowed her to care for herself. Her depression led to more complexity in her life, as she learned to let herself be angry when necessary and forgive when appropriate.

Now, we will look at the symptoms of depression and the specific gifts they have to offer. Subsequent chapters will go into more depth, but the following discussion will offer an understanding of each symptom as representing one sequential stage of personal transformation.

The Stages of Change

Listed below are the symptoms, or stages, of depression reframed as gifts.

Symptom, or Stage, of Depression	The Gift It Offers
Withdrawal, lack of interest, and fatigue	Reorientation
Restlessness, insomnia, and worthlessness	Search for meaning
Thoughts of suicide	Letting go of outworn aspects of one's identity
Grief	Renewal

Emptiness	Enlightened nonattachment
Indifference	Opportunity to overcome conformity
Sadness and self-doubt	Opportunity to break free from approval seeking
Indecisiveness, helplessness, and confusion	Opening to the mysterious

These symptoms, or stages, unfold such that each represents a stepping-stone for further progression toward personal transformation. Let's now review the course these symptoms and stages may take in a depression, and how they can be seen as meaningful.

In the first stage, the withdrawal that characterizes depression is reframed as the necessary catalyst to effect a reorientation. When you realize something has to change, you need to figure out where to go. Retreating from the real world allows for this process of changing directions. The dread and existential angst of depression is reframed as an important search for meaning that will provide a direction for you to follow. As you try to move forward you will confront obstacles within yourself. Depression forces you to let go of parts of yourself that represent obstacles to a meaningful life, which may present themselves in the form of thoughts of suicide. As you let go of central but unhelpful aspects of your identity, you move into reclaiming your grief, and, as you grieve, these new losses evoke earlier losses. As the grief washes away rigid, habitual patterns of defense, you must learn to embrace emptiness in order to clear the way for something new. As you move into a new way of being, not caring what other people think permits you to expand your sense of what is allowable and allows you to experiment with new ways of being in the world. Thus, becoming indifferent to other people's evaluations of you marks a shift in the work of depression from internal to external. The inevitable failures and rejections that follow as you change your way of viewing the world are endured through the humility of depression, which frees you from the need to have approval from the environment. As your life is rebuilt and old plans fall away, you gain a sense of the mysterious and the value of not knowing or controlling the future.

This stage model for personal transformation described above represents a map of sorts, guiding you through a depression. Significant transitions between stages are often signaled by the presence of restlessness, insomnia, fear, and angst. These fearful feelings may be a response to the anxiety that comes with losing control. As you come to understand that something needs to change, you will realize that the world as you know it will be destabilized, and you may begin to experience this fear of losing your known structure. Although the prospect of change is threatening and leads to some of these anxiety-related symptoms, the fear of losing control may actually lead directly to the search for meaning in your life.

REAL-WORLD CHANGE

One of the significant transitions in the journey of depression described above is the movement from internal work to outer work. The retreat, the withdrawal, and many of the painful emotions facilitate an internal reconfiguration of your interests, values, and pursuits. But at some point, transformation requires that you actually do something different.

Some of the symptoms of depression help bring about these changes in the real world. For example, the loss of interest in other people can help you to act in ways that defy their expectations. While a therapist might take a client's statements like "I don't care what anyone thinks" as an ominous sign, they might actually be helping that person make necessary changes in behavior that would be disruptive to their social circle. Similarly, if you feel self-doubt and self-recrimination, these feelings may be signals that you are pushing the limits of what was previously comfortable to you and are creating your own path. In addition, the symptoms of confusion and indecisiveness may reflect a greater openness to experience, so after going through this journey your life will be different because you will live your life with less rigid expectations, and you may have a greater appreciation of the mysteriousness of your life course.

Cast as the stages of a journey, rather than as depressive symptoms, the steps can be seen as follows:

1. Retreat

2. Search for meaning

3. Recognition of parts of self as obstacles to forward movement

4. Washing away or reducing the importance of these obstacles

5. Emptiness

6. Acting in the world in a new way

7. Disconfirmation from the environment

8. Moving forward with greater openness and less rigidity

A person who has gone through this journey will be fundamentally different if he or she has embraced the gifts of each stage. Some of the fundamental changes are noted below.

■ Sarah's Story

One person who followed this path toward transformation was Sarah (adapted from Honos-Webb, Stiles, and Greenberg 2003), who reported a clinical depression and sought help from a therapist. She believed her depression was caused by her sense of isolation related to her recent divorce. Rather than bouncing back and finding new social connections, she found herself retreating more and more from social situations. She reported that she had barriers that prevented her from connecting with others, did not want to connect with others, shut down or froze up in social situations, and found it difficult to communicate.

She sought out therapy in order to heal from her depression but also to find a deeper meaning to her life. She began to explore questions of meaning, such as "Who am I?" "How did I get here?" and "What do I want out of my life?"

In looking for the answers to these questions, she recognized that there were two obstacles preventing her from connecting with other people. One obstacle was her fear of rejection, and the other was a strong message she had been raised with that she should always be suspicious of other people's motives, because they were likely to take advantage of her. In her depression and her search for meaning she realized she was willing to take risks in order to connect with others. She realized that to her a meaningful life was one where she had trusting relationships and social support.

As she realized how much she had lost in her years of maintaining strong barriers to keep others at a distance, she felt grief for the lost relationships and her social isolation. As she felt the grief, she committed herself to take risks to communicate with others, speak her mind, and connect authentically with others.

As she let go of her barriers she felt a sense of emptiness, since her life had been guided by these barriers for so long. The emptiness was compounded by the fact that she had been taught the value and importance of protecting oneself from others by her family. It seemed as if giving up these barriers was separating her from her deepest roots.

As Sarah experienced the stage of emptiness, guided by a therapist, she began taking risks in the real world. She began speaking her mind at work, voicing opinions that she knew others might not approve of. She also began accepting social invitations and reaching out to others.

She experienced many setbacks and some negative feedback about this change in her behavior, causing her to feel self-doubt. She also experienced typical symptoms of confusion and difficulty making decisions. She was acting in new ways, which was liberating and also led to some rejection. However, she was able to recognize that the loss of control she felt about giving up her barriers allowed her to connect more easily with others. She also began to recognize the difference between maintaining boundaries and erecting barriers. In contrast to the barriers, which she had used to keep everyone out, she found that with boundaries she could let some people in and keep others out, and she could choose how much to let people in.

Although this case is an idealized version of the sequence of stages, not everyone will follow these sequences in this order. However, Sarah's story illustrates how the various symptoms and gifts of depression are related to each other. Each person's experience of depression is unique: it may follow a circular path, bounce back and forth between different stages, or skip steps altogether.

The journey through depression results in predictable changes that can be seen as gifts. After going through this journey you will be very different. You will have more internal resources, you will be more flexible, you will be more open to experience, and you will be stronger.

A Gift of Depression: More Internal Resources

After going through a depression you will have more internal complexity. This difference is reflected in the story of Lisa, described earlier, who through her depression moved from believing that "one must always forgive" to recognizing that she had a right to honor her anger and stand up for her rights. Greater complexity means that you will have access to more parts of yourself, and be able to make more choices about your life. Lisa realized that she could choose between being angry or forgiving.

Learning this, Lisa found that she had more tools in her toolbox to help her face life's situations. As a rule, the more complex you are, the more capable you will be of handling life's problems. For example, if you were a handyperson and made your living fixing problems in people's homes, the more tools and resources you had available to you, the more problems you would be able to solve. If all you had was a hammer, you might not be able to help a person who needed a wall repainted. If you had a paint brush, paints, and a hammer, then you could help more people and solve more problems.

The gifts of depression often bring a new way of being into the person's repertoire of interaction. While depression often shows that a part of the self needs to be "cut off," in reality what happens is that this part is given less control or dominance over the personality. For example, Lisa did not actually cut off her desire to forgive as much as she no longer let it dominate all of her interactions. It simply became less important.

A Gift of Depression: More Flexibility

It follows that if you add a new way of being into your repertoire, you will be capable of being more flexible. You have the power to respond differently depending on the situation or the person. Lisa may now choose to forgive a classmate who unknowingly offends her. And she may choose to experience and act on the anger she feels toward her husband when he thoughtlessly expects her to put up with his disrespect. She is capable of choosing different responses rather than just reacting.

Another example of the increased flexibility following depression was the case of Sarah, described earlier. At the end of her therapy she was more flexible in her relations to other people. Rather than rejecting them outright, she had the capacity to use her discrimination but she also had an increased ability to connect with others authentically.

A Gift of Depression: More Openness to Experience

After going through the stages of depression, you will be more capable of tolerating uncertainty and being open to new experiences. Because you may have gone through a breakdown of sorts, your boundaries are now more likely to be permeable and allow new experiences in. Because you have seen some of your fundamental values shift, you are more likely to be open to other people's different values and perspectives.

The period of emptiness you experience during depression may teach you that nature hates a void (meaning that a new experience of the world will likely evolve), and your new ability to tolerate uncertainty may mean that you can give up some measure of control. This change allows you to move toward a more receptive way of being in the world rather than believing that you must make everything happen.

Imagine a person visiting a beautiful natural park in order to go on a specific hike while wearing a pedometer to track the number of miles traveled. Now imagine another person visiting that same natural park. He has a guide in his backpack, but he allows himself to wander around and go to places that seem interesting to him at the moment. Experiencing emptiness during depression will allow you to be more like the spontaneous hiker. This less-focused, less-controlling way of being in the world can in fact open up more opportunities to you since you are able to take advantage of uncharted territory and impulses and instincts that arise.

A Gift of Depression: Increased Strength

After you go through a depression you will be better able to cope with life events. People turn away from difficult inner and outer experiences because they feel overwhelmed by them. A person can face experiences and problems that he feels he can manage. The more complex, flexible, and open a person is, the more he is capable of bearing experiences. Some people cannot bear experiences that they are not fully in control of; for example, people may leave relationships if they find that their partners have a will of their own. Going through a depression may help a person learn to tolerate uncertainty and complexity and give up some measure of control, which allows him to be stronger.

OBSTACLES TO TRANSFORMING DEPRESSION INTO A GIFT

As with any journey or path, you can expect to find obstacles that will make you doubt your efforts to find the gifts in your depression. And as is the case with obstacles in any situation, the ability to predict them and plan how you will manage them will increase the likelihood of success in transforming your depression. Below are some predictable obstacles that you may encounter in your efforts to heal from depression.

Fear of Losing Control

The fundamental gift of depression is its role as a signal telling you that something new needs to come into your life. Any time significant change happens in yourself and in your life, you can expect to experience a fear of losing control. This fear happens because you are entering into unknown territory and you are losing a connection to familiar ground. If you open yourself to new experiences you are also giving up some measure of control, which predictably leads to fear.

The best way to handle the fear that will inevitably appear is to interpret it as a signal of that new something coming into your life. You should not interpret the fear as an intensification of your depressive symptoms and assume that now you have an anxiety disorder to go with your depressive disorder. Rather, the fear necessarily accompanies the effort to heal from depression by honoring the life-changing messages in the depression.

This shift in understanding fear has also been understood in larger societal terms by authors Frances Lappé and Jeff Perkins, who argue that our evolutionary development requires a different understanding of fear. They write that "our future may depend on whether we can achieve a radical shift in our inherited view of fear, whether we can learn to see fear with new eyes. Rather than a warning that something is wrong, fear in certain circumstances can come to mean that something is just right, that we're doing precisely what is true to our deepest wisdom" (Lappé and Perkins 2004, p. 15). If you can interpret your fear about the changes in your life as indicating that something new and important is coming in and encouraging you to keep going in that direction, you will avoid the obstacle of being stopped by the inevitable fear that arises in the face of change.

Phobia of Emotions

Another obstacle that can prevent you from finding the gifts of depression is a phobia of your emotional life. Many of the gifts that emerge from depression include the capacity to feel more deeply and experience a wider range of emotions. A depression can lead to an increased capacity to feel angry and set boundaries, and also an increased desire to connect with others and feel tenderness. Each emotion must be felt to be used as a guide in redirecting your life. Because these emotions are powerful, they can be scary and sometimes cause you to fear them. The best way to confront this obstacle is to prepare yourself and expect to confront emotions that are uncomfortable. By understanding that the gift is in the emotion and by reminding yourself that you will not drown in your emotions—that you will always be able to find a way out—you will be prepared to handle this potential obstacle.

Depression as a Bad Habit

If you have been depressed for a long time, it can become a habit that is hard to break. You may have forgotten what it feels like to be not depressed. Paradoxically, healing from depression may be uncomfortable to you because it represents new territory. One way to prepare for this obstacle is to remind yourself that you deserve to be free from this habit and that you would rather be afraid than depressed. As we've discussed earlier, even positive changes will bring with them fear and a sense of losing control. As you bring awareness to the process of changing your life, the choice you need to make between comfortable depression and the unknown will be obvious.

Depression as an Attachment

One obstacle to healing from depression is the attachment to and identification with a loved one who is depressed. When a person has grown up in a family where a parent or sibling was significantly depressed, he may identify with the loved one through the feelings of depression. If this is the case, then letting go of the depression is terribly threatening because it may feel like letting go of the parent or sibling. For example, a woman who is depressed and whose mother is or was depressed may use the depression as a means of maintaining her connection to her mother, and she may feel that she would be abandoning her mother by letting go of the depression. The best way to confront this obstacle is to consider whether it applies to you, and stay aware of it. If you have a depressed relative you are deeply attached to, you may want to confront this obstacle by telling yourself that the best thing you can give to that person is to make your own life work. Your happiness is always a gift to those who care deeply for you.

Secondary Gains of Depression

Another obstacle to finding the gifts of depression in your own life might be the secondary gains that come with being depressed. In other words, you are rewarded for being depressed in some way. These rewards, or gains, may be fairly obvious. It may be that other people solve your problems for you because they want to protect you from too much stress, or that family members protect you from conflict because they don't want to make your depression worse. Depression may even be giving you an excuse to not go to work.

In other cases the secondary gains may be more subtle. Some clients have discovered that by being depressed they get to show their abusive parents how miserably they failed in their parenting ("Look how miserable I am—you really messed up as a parent"). The best way to prepare for this obstacle is to examine your life for any benefits you may be gaining from being depressed. If you find that you do receive rewards, even small ones, for staying depressed, you should ask yourself whether those rewards are worth the price of staying depressed.

EXERCISE: IS IT WORTH IT?

1. In your journal, make a list of rewards you get from your depression. You do not need to feel embarrassed or ashamed about these rewards. Any behavior, thought, emotion, or condition will have costs and benefits. In this exercise, you are just practicing becoming aware of what the benefits of your depression might be. List as many benefits or rewards as possible.

2. Choose the three most powerful benefits. Which benefits seem compelling to you? Which benefits would be hard to live without?

3. As you look at these benefits, ask yourself, "Is it worth it to stay depressed in order to maintain these benefits?" In your journal, write your response to this question. You might be surprised to find that your knee-jerk response is yes. If that's the case, just keep writing and don't censor what you think and feel.

4. Return to the list of the three most-powerful benefits. Write each one in your journal, followed by the question "How can I get this benefit without being depressed?" Come up with as many answers as possible, even if they don't make sense yet or you can't see how they would really work. For example, one client said that he could obtain the benefit of showing his parents what a failure they were by just telling them that they were miserable failures as parents.

5. Look at your list of ideas from step 4, and create an action plan to help you work toward achieving these benefits in your life without being depressed.

A thorough review of these obstacles will help you prepare to reframe specific symptoms of depression as meaningful communications about changing your life. You will have much more success in transforming your depression—and being transformed by it—if you are prepared to meet and deal with the obstacles that will surely arise. Let's now look at each symptom in turn and examine its message to you, beginning with withdrawal, loss of interest, and fatigue.

Chapter 3

Depression as a Reorientation

In this chapter we switch from exploring the general idea of depression as a gift to revealing the specific gifts of concrete symptoms. One of the defining features, or symptoms, of depression is a loss of interest in one's day-to-day life. What used to be meaningful no longer is. Social relationships that once were enchanting now seem like an energy drain. Hobbies and other pursuits seem like a waste of time. Professional activities feel like a meaningless grind. It is this loss of interest and attendant withdrawal that often causes the greatest impairment in functioning. Romantic relationships and friendships are strained. Professional failures often result from lack of interest and motivation. Family members suffer as they worry that you might be ruining your life.

In addition to the loss of interest, the symptom of fatigue also promotes a withdrawal from one's life. Fatigue can be so extreme that even thinking about doing laundry may be impossible. Some people with depression want to sleep most of the day and find it hard to do the simplest chores or even maintain proper hygiene. Others make it to work and back, only to collapse in front of the TV every evening, virtually unable to move for entire weekends.

It may seem hard to imagine how this withdrawal from one's life, this impairment of functioning, can be a gift. Most psychologists and mental health providers assume that such a withdrawal from life and increased sense of meaninglessness can only mean one thing: a profound psychological disorder.

This conclusion is based on the premise, mentioned earlier, that the life a person lives before she experiences depression is the gold standard and that the goal of treatment is to return her to her previous level of functioning. But what if this premise is wrong? What if a person's previous level of functioning was off track? If one considers that there might have been something wrong with her previous way of being in the world, then a depression might be thought of as a withdrawal from that life as a way to envision a new life path.

In her book *Everything Happens for a Reason*, Mira Kirshenbaum (2004) writes that bad things happen so that individuals will become their best, most authentic self:

> Things happen to help you get rid of the parts of yourself that aren't you; to help you be more real and more yourself, not like everyone else; to help you lead a more authentic life; and ultimately to help you discover who you really are. Circumstances often take us away from who we really are. And the further we drift, the more likely that it's going to take some final loss or difficulty to shove in our faces the fact that we don't even know who we are anymore. This helps us wake up so we can once again rediscover our true selves. (p. 22)

Although her book addressed the issue of finding meaning in painful events and losses, her approach is relevant to depression, which can reorient you to your deepest, best, most authentic self.

WHY DO PEOPLE GET OFF TRACK?

Before we elaborate on the ways depression is a signal that one has gotten off track, it is worth exploring the question of how and why people get off track in the first place. But what track have they strayed from? One way to understand this is to think of people you know who have gotten themselves into situations that are an obvious mismatch for them. For example, an artistic person who works in a Fortune 500 company purely for job security, and a person who has gotten married for the wrong reasons, are examples of people who are off track. Below, we will explore some of the reasons individuals make choices that are not in their own interest.

Conformity

One of the main reasons you might make a choice that is out of line with your own real interests and desires is the need to conform to the expectations of others. Parents' expectations often set a person on a particular life course without their realizing it. Let's look at Sue's experience. Sue was an attractive woman whose family had impressed on her from a young age that she needed to marry into a prominent family and elevate her own family's social status. Sue's love for her family, and their strong expectations of her, served to direct her life path toward attracting a mate with high social status. Much of her life energy was directed toward this goal. It was only after an experience of depression that Sue began to reflect on her own real needs and interests and to question whether her parents' expectations were appropriate for directing her life course.

During her depression she stopped dating because she became so negative and hopeless about finding someone she deeply cared about. This allowed her to realize that the pressure to fulfill her parents' expectations had impaired her ability to find a relationship. She understood that the enormous pressure she felt was preventing her from having a good time dating, and that she had probably been rejecting people she might really enjoy. By selecting men who fulfilled her parents' expectations she had been dating men who had values that differed from her own. She was most interested in social activism, while the men who met her parents' expectations for social mobility were usually so absorbed in their professional life that they didn't think at all about deeper issues such as social justice.

Expectations of conformity may also come from friends, peers, media, or other larger cultural forces. For example, some women may feel an intense pressure to get married and have children and may never stop to consider whether such a path is really what they want. A woman whose deepest interests lie in exploring the world may find the life of a mother and wife to be unbearable. Even a woman who is in touch with her own needs may find the cultural expectations about marriage and motherhood to be overwhelming. A woman who is trying to meet cultural expectations at the expense of her own internal desires may fall prey to an insidious depression, which would then provide her with an opportunity to reflect on her own needs.

Need for Security

Another reason you might ignore your own internal signals is that the need for security can overpower your own sense of what is essentially meaningful. We see this in the person who marries for money, but it can manifest itself in many other ways. You might make career choices solely because of their promise of financial security, for example. The need for security can take other forms, such as staying in relationships that are familiar or safe, or failing to take necessary risks to make one's dreams come true.

Sometimes depression makes you miserable in your current lifestyle in order to make it clear to you that the comfort of familiarity also comes with a price. Depression can serve as an inducement for taking risks. You begin to realize that though there are costs involved in moving away from security, the cost of not taking any risks is already a high price to pay. As Danish philosopher Søren Kierkegaard has written, "to risk is to lose your footing for a while. Not to risk is to lose your life" (Caddy and Platts 1992).

In some instances a person's great gifts can turn against them, allowing them to succeed in fields for which they are completely ill suited. Shannon was intellectually brilliant, with an adventuresome personality, a deep sensitivity toward others, and a need for connections. When she found herself facing graduation without a clear direction, she decided to apply for law school. She was easily accepted into a top school, won top honors as a student, and was offered a job at a prestigious and well-paying firm. Because her intelligence allowed her so much success and offered the opportunity of lifelong financial security, it was hard for her to hear her inner voice telling her that she was not interested in spending her life as a lawyer.

Everyone has a need for security. It is only when the need for security overshadows your own interests and needs that it can take your life off track.

Not Feeling Good Enough

Low self-esteem can also cause you to allow your life to go off track. Perhaps you don't feel good enough about yourself to follow your real interests and passions. For instance, like many people who marry for money or social status, there are individuals who do not pursue passionate love interests because they do not feel they are good enough for the other person. And, like many people who take jobs just for the money and prestige, there are those who do not pursue their real talents and gifts because they don't think they are good enough to succeed.

Sheldon always wanted to be a doctor. His mother spent most of her life sick and disabled and he always thought he wanted to understand how the body worked so he could heal others. He had the intelligence to succeed as a doctor, and he possessed a natural, easy manner that would have served his patients. But because of his father, an alcoholic who was habitually unemployed, Sheldon decided that being a doctor was not for him. He thought he just wasn't in that league, both intellectually and because of the shame he felt about his family. His belief that doctors had to come from good families took him off track, away from his true professional calling.

Need for Approval

You might also find your life directed by the need for approval rather than by your own inner values, needs, and desires. While it is true that everyone really does need approval and a sense of community, a need for approval that is out of balance can cause you to live your life doing what will make others like you. Jan regularly put others' needs ahead of her own (Honos-Webb et al. 1998). Her clients always came first in her sales job. Her husband's needs came first at home. She dutifully fulfilled her family's demands that she take care of her parents. Soon it became clear that she had lost a sense of who she was; she was disconnected from her own wants, needs, values, and desires.

When a person's efforts to gain approval from others gets this far out of balance, a depression predictably results (Joiner et al. 2001).

Unfortunately, living a life driven by the need for approval often doesn't give you the fulfillment you so fervently hope for. Instead, you end up like a doormat, constantly feeling taken advantage of because of your inability to set limits. You lose the respect of others rather than winning their approval.

If the paragraphs above describe your experience, you may find yourself angry at the very people whose needs you are catering to. This anger creates a feeling of conflict within you. And the more conflicted you feel, the more afraid you become of expressing your real self. As a result, you may drive your feelings deeper underground, becoming more and more disconnected from who you really are—straying farther and farther from the life you're meant to lead.

Fear

Sometimes people know exactly what they want to do and who they want to be, but their deep fears prevent them from following their internal compass. While fear may be related to many of the other forces that drive a person off track, such as fear of losing security, it can also be much broader in nature. The authors of *You Have the Power: Choosing Courage in a Culture of Fear* argue that our entire culture is steeped in fear (Lappé and Perkins 2004). You may simply fear doing something different than you have done before. Then there are all the businesses that market their products by making you aware of everything you have to lose and all the things that can go wrong—insurance companies whose ads warn of all the hazards of life without an umbrella policy, for example. It can be hard to trust your own voice when there are so many voices in the media telling you how scary life can be.

Another example of the pervasive anxiety promoted in our culture is seen in the importance placed on being thin. Women who are constantly exposed to media images of the thin ideal may find themselves fearful of getting fat. While most people don't think of a woman who spends a great deal of her time exercising and obsessing about food and weight as a great tragedy, the extent of the loss can be seen when you think about what she is not doing or thinking about in her efforts to maintain her low weight. Very often, her fear of being fat has prevented her from finding and fulfilling her own dreams. As you can see, a life driven by fear and spent avoiding that which is feared can get profoundly off track as the person loses connection with all but the efforts to ward off the feared events.

Lack of Deep Reflection

It might be that you have become disconnected from who you are and gotten off track simply by not reflecting on what you really want from life. It's not that you are out of balance; it's just easier to go with the flow. An example of this person might be someone who gets married to the first person who proposes to her. She likes him well enough and does not reflect deeply about this profound life choice and is happy to reach this developmental milestone without much searching. Another example might be the person who falls into the family business without exploring other options. In these cases, it's not that anything has gone wrong; it's just that the person does what is easiest without reflecting deeply on how closely her internal talents and values match the opportunities that present themselves. When depression hits, it can be seen as a breakdown that provides an opportunity for a breakthrough—a chance to reflect and get one's life back on track.

DEPRESSION AS A BREAKDOWN

One thing that is sure to get us to do some deep reflection is a breakdown. For example, if your life is going along smoothly, you probably won't spend time thinking about its meaning. But when something stops working, then you're much more likely to think deeply about life; when we identify a problem, we begin to reflect on what caused the problem and how to fix it. So, if you are disconnected from your deepest feelings and impulses, you may still manage to get through life without realizing it—if nothing goes wrong, that is.

One of the defining features of depression is that it results in impairment in social and professional functioning. You may feel blue and begin to lose interest in some aspects of your life, but this will not be diagnosed as depression unless it begins to impair your day-to-day functioning. It is this aspect of depression—which is by definition an impairment—that seems the most difficult to reconcile with the idea that depression is a gift.

But if you begin to accept the possibility that there was something fundamentally wrong with your level of functioning before your depression, the idea of depression as a gift begins to make sense. A breakdown can become a gift when it leads to increasing reflection on your life, which will in turn lead you to ask these fundamentally important questions:

- What is wrong with my life?

- What can I do to correct the problem?

The importance of these questions, and the impact of deep reflection on your life course, can be seen in Matt's stories below.

■ Matt's Story

Matt came from a loving, working-class family. His family made sacrifices so that he could get the best education possible. He did well in school and was the first person in his family to go to college. Matt calculated that the best way to make the most money with the least education (i.e., without going to graduate school) was to get a degree at a business school. He figured that after four years he would be in a good position to make money and escape his working-class background. He was accepted into the business school and succeeded there.

MATT: A LIFE WITHOUT DEPRESSION

After graduation Matt went to work in a large New York corporation as an accountant, making more money than both of his parents together had ever made. He spent most of his time at work working with numbers and budgets. His financial success and easygoing personality made him attractive to women, and he married a woman who he felt was a catch because she came from a privileged background and was very well connected socially. They had children, and Matt spent most of his time working hard to maintain the lifestyle his wife was accustomed to. Matt's life was comfortable, and from the outside it seemed he had everything he had always wanted. Although sometimes he felt as if life was passing him by, or that something was missing, in general he didn't have many complaints.

MATT: A LIFE WITH DEPRESSION

After graduation Matt went to work in a large New York corporation as an accountant, making more money than both of his parents together had ever made. However, after two years he began to feel depressed. He spent a lot of time at work procrastinating, surfing the Web, and planning his fantasy football team rather than keeping up with his accounting work. When he came home from work he would drink a few beers and sit in front of the TV. He was dating a woman who came from a privileged background, but even though she lived a lifestyle he and his family had only dreamed of, he still found himself not wanting to commit to her. He couldn't understand why he had so many doubts about this seemingly perfect woman.

His depression was causing impairments in both his professional life and his relationship. His supervisor told him that he was not working up to par and put him on probation. His girlfriend told him that if he could not make a commitment she would begin to date other people. His life was falling apart. He began to ask himself what was wrong with his life. He used to be so easygoing, but now everything was a struggle. Upon reflection, he realized that he didn't really like his job. He didn't like the monotony of working with minutiae and doing calculations all day and craved more social contact. He realized he would rather spend his time working with people than numbers and that he wanted to work in sports or entertainment.

Matt decided to figure out what other career options might be more in line with his real interests. He began to research what sorts of jobs were available in the sports industry, and he discovered that he might be able to work at a sports news channel, where he could combine his interests in sports and entertainment. He left his high-salary job and took a lower-paying position as a researcher for a major sports news channel, and he found that he loved every minute of his work life. His girlfriend left him because of his decreased earning power and his struggle with commitment, but he found himself surrounded by people who loved sports as much as he did and who spent their work hours doing what they loved. He met a production assistant who was artistic, down to earth, and as enthuasiast about sports as he was, and they spent their free time attending sporting events and hob-nobbing with athletes. After a year or so, he married his girl-friend and they had children together. Eventually, with his wife's coaching and encouragement, he achieved his dream of becoming a sports newscaster on a cable sports news channel.

A TALE OF TWO MATTS

As these two vignettes demonstrate, the impairment caused by Matt's depression was significant and resulted in failure in both his work life and his love life. But it also caused him to reflect on his problems and reoriented him to a completely new life. The rewards of the new life were so fulfilling that the breakdown itself became just a fleeting memory and a blessing in disguise. His entire life shifted course for the better once he heard the message that his depression was communicating.

The gift of Matt's depression was a deeply fulfilling life. In the version of his life without depression, life was good, but it wasn't great. Because there was nothing seriously wrong with that life he might never have been motivated to seek to fulfill his deepest desires, unless depression were to come along and stop him in his tracks, so he could get back on track toward a great life.

REORIENTATION: AWAY FROM WEAKNESS, TOWARD STRENGTHS

Matt's case illustrates one of the fundamental reorientations that can be put in motion by a depression: a shift from patching up weaknesses toward finding and using your strengths. In Matt's case, his strengths were his love of sports and his easy personality. Both of these served him in his new career as a sports broadcaster. Extensive Gallup polling has demonstrated that the tendency to focus one's time and energy on identifying, investigating, and trying to patch up weaknesses is a world-wide trend. Marcus Buckingham and Donald Clifton (2001) report that individuals around the world are fixated on improving their weaknesses rather than on a deep understanding of their strengths as the path to self-improvement. These authors argue that people become fixated on weaknesses because of their education and upbringing; their research shows that parents acknowledge focusing more on their children's areas of weakness (such as failing in algebra) than on their strengths (getting an A in social studies) in an effort to prepare their children for the competitiveness of the education system.

If the psychologist Carl Jung was correct in his assessment that "criticism has the power to do good when there is something that must be destroyed, dissolved or reduced, but it is capable only of great harm when there is something to be built" (Buckingham and Clifton 2001, p. 124), then the implications of this intense focus on correcting weaknesses rather than building strengths is worrisome. A child's confidence is clearly something to be built and one can hardly keep from wondering if there is a connection between the increasing competitiveness of the American school system, the focus on weakness, and the increasing rates of depression in children and adolescents.

The focus on weaknesses is also an ingrained part of the model in which mental health professionals are trained and therefore pass on to their clients. So, when you go to a psychologist asking for help with your depression, you are likely to be given a depressing diagnosis with a depressing prognosis and asked to delve deeply into all the good reasons you have for getting depressed in the first place. Often you will be given the depressing feedback that you are biologically hardwired to be and stay depressed.

However, if you or your psychologist identifies the depression as an effort to reorient yourself toward a life that uses your strengths and minimizes focus on weaknesses, then you can transform your life and find the gift within the depression.

Reorientation: Toward Self-Care

Depression helps you shift away from taking care of others and toward taking care of yourself. Many of the examples we've looked at so far illustrate this. Jan shifted from putting her customers, husband, and family first to putting herself first. Lisa shifted from solving the problems her husband caused with his gambling toward figuring out how to get her own life on track. Matt shifted from fulfilling his family's dreams of upward mobility to easing into a comfortable life of sports and fun that allowed him to use his natural abilities.

As you withdraw your life energy from your current life, you may find that your family members, friends, and mental health providers become very worried about you. They don't see that on the other side of this withdrawal is a new life course. However, once you understand depression as a way of changing the course of your life, it makes sense that you would need to withdraw, or retreat, from your daily life, so that you can connect with who and what you are. Richard Bach has said that "what the caterpillar calls the end of the world, the master calls a butterfly" (1989, p. 169). The following exercises will help you to see your depression not as the end of the world but instead as a retreat that allows you to open up new possibilities in your life. While this chapter is intended to help you identify and overcome the obstacles that have kept you off track, the next chapter will help you begin to chart the new direction that may emerge if the reorientation is successfully navigated.

EXERCISE: IS IT WORTH IT TO BE A CATERPILLAR?

This exercise is based on Richard Bach's description of cocooning, or what we are calling a retreat, as the vehicle for a transformation. To the caterpillar, retreating into the dark and limited cocoon may indeed seem like the end of the world. Inside, it is cut off from its familiar world so that it may experience a total transformation. In this exercise we explore whether the benefits of the transformation are worth the effort to retreat into a dark and unfamiliar cocoon.

1. Earlier in this chapter, we identified the obstacles that may cause a person's life to go off track:

    ■   Pressure to conform

    ■   Need for security

- Not feeling good enough

- Need for approval

- Fear

- Lack of deep reflection

Now, take out your journal. Ask yourself which of these potential obstacles, or barriers, seems to be the biggest problem for you. For example, if pressure to conform is your major obstacle, write down the answers to "How is my life affected by my need for conformity?" Let yourself free-associate about this question and then list as many examples as possible of specific behaviors that you do in seeking conformity. For example, one stay-at-home mother found herself writing about the pressure to be a perfect mom and began to recognize the many expectations placed on her that did not fit who she really was. She realized that, in conforming to societal expectations of mothers and trying so hard to be a good mom, she wound up listening to music she did not like, dressing in a way that didn't fit her personality, and attending classes she was not really interested in. She came to the conclusion that unless she changed her life, her children would never know who she really was.

2. Ask yourself the question "How would my life be different if I could have my obstacle surgically removed from my life and being?" However, please keep in mind that getting rid of your need for conformity, security, or approval, for example, would not necessarily be a good thing! All of these needs are genuine and authentic. It would be very destructive if you really could cut out these very human needs. They only become a problem when they get out of balance and begin to be the primary force driving a person's life. So you will ultimately want to hang on to your needs for conformity, security, and approval, but you will want to downgrade them to preferences rather than keeping them as the driving factors in your life.

In your journal, write your reflections on the question given above. Be creative and explore all the ways your life would be different if you did not have your particular obstacle. For example, the stay-at-home mother mentioned above wrote that, freed of the need to conform to others' expectations, she would enroll her youngest child in day care a few hours a week so she could pursue her interests in yoga and Latin dance, she would listen to soul music in the car rather than her children's tapes, and she would allow herself to dress more flamboyantly.

3.   In this step you will use your journal to reflect on the costs and benefits of your personal obstacle. Draw a line down the middle of one page and write "Costs of My Obstacle" on the left-hand side and "Benefits of My Obstacle" on the right-hand side. (Feel free to substitute the name of your own obstacle, such as "Fear" or "Need for Approval," for "My Obstacle" in these headings). For example, the stay-at-home mother who had identified conformity as her personal obstacle wrote that the costs of this obstacle were boredom with her life, unauthentic relationships with other moms, and her children not really knowing her real personality. Her benefits of her obstacle were that she was easily accepted by other moms, she didn't have to risk her husband's complaints about the cost of part-time day care, and she didn't have to risk rejection for dressing to fit her personality.

4.   Evaluate your assessment of the risks and benefits of your need for your personal obstacle. Pick one change you could make in your life that moves you away from this obstacle and toward your more authentic needs and desires. Ask yourself the following questions:

■   What do I need in order to make this change in my life?

■   What can I do now to make this change?

■   Who can support me in making this change?

■   When will I make this change?

Write down a specific and concrete plan. Give yourself a deadline by which you'll have succeeded in taking two steps toward your goal.

5.   Be mindful of keeping a balance between your need to cling to your personal obstacle and your need to venture outside the bounds of this obstacle. Create a plan that fits with your lifestyle and pacing to implement some of the other changes you wrote about in step 2. You don't want to rush ahead and overturn your

life by changing everything all at once. For example, each week, make just one small exploration outside the bounds of your need for conformity.

6.   After each experiment trying a new behavior that frees you from your personal obstacle, write about the positive and negative consequences of your actions. Continue to evaluate the changes, and choose directions that yield the most positive consequences and that do not create more problems than they solve. If something happens that you did not expect, such as criticism from a partner, you can either pick a different behavior to try or practice standing your ground with the new behavior. You can use your internal feelings as a compass to help you figure out which course you take. If you feel increasingly paralyzed by the conflict, then you can choose a less-ambitious behavior. If you feel energized, then you can begin to practice asking others to accommodate the changes you are making.

7.   You can choose to repeat this exercise with any or all of the obstacles (see step 1 in this exercise) that may have driven your life off track and led to the depression.

8.   After you have recognized the obstacles that have taken you off track, you are able to better understand your loss of interest and fatigue as a retreat that will help you begin the process of reorienting your life. Earlier we suggested that reorientation often helps a person learn (1) to live based on his or her strengths rather than weaknesses and (2) to reorient toward taking care of the self rather than focusing on others. You may want to spend some time writing in your journal about which of these reorientations you are undergoing. Perhaps both shifts are taking place in you. Take some time to brainstorm and generate as many possibilities as you can about what you might be moving away from in your retreat. Ask yourself the following questions:

■   What is wrong with my life?

■   What can I do to correct the problem?

Record your answers in your journal.

FEELING BLUE'S CLUES

The nature of your symptoms gives you clues to how to change your life. The more blue you feel, the more changes you can expect. The area of your life most affected by the depression will be the area of your life most in need of change.

As a general rule, you can expect that the intensity of the symptoms will mirror the intensity of the message that requires your attention. The more serious the depression, the more urgent the message is to be heard. The farther a person has come from his or her own nature, the more urgent the message to get back on track. Alternatively, a person suffering a low-grade, temporary depression may simply need to do some problem solving rather than overhaul everything. For example, an artist fulfilling her true calling may find that she really wants to switch from painting to sculpting. The changes indicated in her depression are less dramatic than those an artistically talented person might need to make if she were working in a computer programming job. Therefore, if you find yourself with a mild depression and yet feel a sense that you are on the right track, you may need to make only some minor adjustments, which will lead you to even more fulfillment.

In a similar way, you can examine your symptoms for clues about what part of your life they are pointing toward. If, for example, you find that you have lost interest in all of your friendships but not in your romantic partner, this may indicate that you need to examine the area of your life that includes your circle of friends. If your loss of interest pertains only to your professional life, then that is likely the domain that needs deep reflection so you can increase your awareness of current problems. By tracking the intensity of your symptoms and the area of your life where your symptoms are most disruptive, you can gain clues about the extent of the changes that are needed and the area of your life that requires the most attention.

Chapter 4

Depression as a Search for Meaning

The pain of depression drives you to search for the deeper meaning of your life. First depression stops you in your tracks, making it difficult for you to continue with your current life. Then depression makes you agonize about what you should do with your life. In this way, it sets you on the path toward greater meaning.

The feelings of worthlessness that are the hallmark of depression may also direct the search for meaning. The feelings are not an accurate reflection of your true value; instead, they are a force that compels you to find a way of living that will be more meaningful and intrinsically valuable. No person is worthless, but it may be that the way you spend your time and energy is worthless relative to your deepest gifts and values. This chapter will show you how to ask these feelings for directions in charting your new course. You will learn how to reframe the symptoms of agitation, worthlessness, and insomnia as ways to motivate your search for meaning.

AGITATION

The symptoms of restlessness and agitation are meant to make you feel uneasy. Agitation is a state of not being able to accept who you are, what you are, and where you are in your life. It is meant to be an important communication to you, intended to get you to search for relief in the form of deeper satisfaction and meaning in your life. Restlessness means that there is something fundamentally wrong in some area of your life and you need to begin searching for what is wrong and figure out how to do it differently.

Because restlessness and agitation provide such a strong impetus to begin the search for something more, psychotherapeutic and spiritual approaches that allow you to self-medicate or dull the agitation may just prolong the symptoms. As a general rule, symptoms will intensify until their message is heard. Some spiritual disciplines that make you feel bad if you haven't achieved a state of inner peace may lead people to use spiritual exercises to alleviate the agitation without fully understanding the reason for the agitation. Similarly, over-the-counter pharmaceuticals or prescription drugs that temporarily take the edge off may actually prolong and intensify these symptoms. While having a glass of wine each night may not indicate a drinking problem, if it distracts you from your agitation and keeps you from translating its message into meaningful action, then this seemingly innocuous habit may be maintaining your depression. The same is true of all the ways of masking depression that were mentioned in the first chapter, including overeating and compulsive busyness.

Existential Dread

A caricature of a person with existential angst is the philosophy student who wears a black turtleneck and smokes cigarettes in a coffee house while reading tomes on "the meaning of meaning" and writing in his journal. Another might be the adolescent struggling to forge an independent identity, asking "Who am I?" "Where am I going?" and "How do I fit in the world?"

It may be that the symptom of agitation is meant to drive you to exactly this sort of exploration and reflection about the meaning of your life. Perhaps our culture's negative stereotype of people engaged in deep examination of their life's purpose leads us to view these experiences as symptoms. It may be that the culture's emphasis on materialism, consumerism, and achievement have relegated the most human of all pursuits—the search for life's meaning—into a symptom to be eliminated.

The term "dread," which originated in existential philosophies, refers to a profound sense of anxiety about the meaning of one's life. It goes along with restlessness and agitation and haunts the person, constantly reminding him that he may be missing something essential in his life—and that life is short. Dread may feel like a heavy, fetid ball in the pit of one's stomach. It may be the sense that "something wicked this way comes." Or the sense that nothing exciting will ever this way come. Dread provokes existential speculation, making philosophers of us all, calling us to reflect and examine who we are, prompting us to reorient ourselves for the journey forward.

Life Is Messy

While existential philosophers considered the experience of dread to be an appropriate reaction to the human predicament, we have now come to think of it as representing something gone wrong. Such a view seems to hold up a sterilized emotional life as the norm for psychological health. Perhaps such a view represents a denial of the existential realities of life where loss, failure, conflict, illness, and death are fundamental realities. The psychological ideal of facing life always with self-possession and poise does not allow for the reality that life is messy. It does not acknowledge that any person facing significant life challenges could be expected to suffer "impairments in functioning"—the clinical standard for diagnosing a mental illness. This current standard of mental health may be related to the medical model, which defines any difference as a disorder and offers medications for modulating differences. According to this model, if you feel too bad (depression) or too good (mania), then you need to employ chemicals to get rid of these deviations. In turn, the ease of access to mood-altering prescription drugs may have led to the creation of this unrealistic standard, which many see as the new "normal."

In short, many cultural factors have made it very difficult for us to tolerate our sense of dread or anxiety in the face of life's uncertainties. Such intolerance of dread may lead us to make choices that cause us to live out of line with our own desires and needs. Even the eminent existential psychologist Irvin Yalom had his own struggle with meaning and authenticity late in his life. He recounts the experience of having a dream in which he is about to die. He sees his mother and calls out to her, "Momma, Momma, how'd I do?" This dream prompts him to ask himself, "Was it possible . . . that I had been conducting my whole life with the primary goal of obtaining my mother's approval?" (Yalom 2002, p. 134). If existential dread prompts you to explore the possibility of aligning your life with your own inner direction, then it may truly have a gift to offer. Truly experiencing and exploring the message in the dread may help to get your life back on track.

EXERCISE: BECOME A DREAD HEAD

Many of the activities you use to distract yourself from the feeling of restless agitation are actually meaningless activities that serve the sole function of helping you to avoid this experience. This exercise will help you begin to tolerate your restlessness and agitation, which we are reframing as an existential dread, or the search for meaning in your life.

This exercise is based on the standard cognitive behavioral strategy known as "graded exposure." In this exercise you will be asked to increase your exposure to the experience of restless dread. You will start out at low, easily managed levels and gradually increase the level of exposure, thereby increasing your ability to tolerate the experience of dread. The purpose of increasing your ability to tolerate dread is twofold: (1) it will allow you to listen for the message in the symptom and (2) it will help you to stop compulsive activities or habits that let you avoid or stamp out the restless agitation.

If you do not think that you experience restless agitation, then this exercise may not be for you. Each depressed person experiences his own patterns of symptoms, and most people do not have all the symptoms of depression. However, this exercise may be worth trying for one or two days, to give yourself a chance to listen for the dread in case you are unwittingly masking it with some behavior.

1. Over the course of two days, observe your levels of restless agitation and just be aware of how it comes and goes. You may want to write in your journal about your observations, rather like a park ranger or naturalist tracking the comings and goings of an animal.

Consider the following questions while observing your restless agitation:

- What happens before I experience restless agitation?

- What do I do as soon as I feel the restless agitation?

- How do I avoid this feeling?

- Are there things I do that make the restless agitation more intense?

- Are there things I do that make the restless agitation less intense?

- Do I have any control over the restless agitation?

2. After two days of just observing your restless agitation, set aside five minutes where you will just feel the full intensity of the restless agitation without trying to make it go away. Do this for as many days as necessary, until you can comfortably sit with restless agitation for five minutes, experiencing it fully without distracting yourself.

3. Now, over the next two days, notice every time your agitation appears, and try to sit with it for five minutes. Write in your journal about the experience of tolerating restless agitation. Write about what you do to avoid the feeling when the five minutes is up. On occasions when you fail to make it to five minutes, write what you did to get away from the feeling. Make a list of all the activities and internal thoughts or strategies you use to minimize or move away from restless agitation.

4. Continue to practice tolerating restless agitation whenever it comes up until you can comfortably experience it for ten minutes at a time.

5. Repeat step 3, sitting instead for ten minutes each time, and then writing about the experience.

6. Repeat step 3 once again, sitting instead for fifteen minutes each time, and then writing about the experience.

7. When you have achieved the ability to tolerate restless agitation and dread for fifteen minutes, you can now begin the process of listening to your dread for its message about your life. To do this, you'll need to "turn up the volume" on the experience by actually making it more intense. To intensify your experience, ask yourself the following questions:

- Where in my body do I feel the restless agitation?

- What does it feel like? Does it feel like battery acid, or is it sharp and icy? (Try to put words to the experience.)

- How big is it?

- Is it rough or smooth?

- Is it tight or loose?

- What color is the feeling?

- Is it a large pressure or a gaping hole?

8. In this practice session, see what sorts of internal statements you make when feeling the dread. Once you have a clear, strong feeling of the existential dread, listen to it—the internal statements you hear may in fact be the dread talking. Translate those messages into a positive action plan. Here are some examples:

Susan found that she often tried to avoid her dread by thinking of eating: what she needed to eat, what she wanted to eat, what she should eat. On many occasions she just ate without thinking. When she increased her capacity to tolerate the dread she found herself saying to herself, "You know how to lose weight; you just refuse to follow the rules." She turned what seemed to be a condemning statement of herself into a positive action plan: "Refuse to follow the rules." She realized that she was meant to apply this plan to her career as an actress. She had been struggling to succeed in her field, but her positive action plan made her realize that she would need to do something edgy and creative in order to make a breakthrough in this industry. She had the skill, the talent, and the discipline, but she was being too careful and she wasn't experiencing the success she had hoped for. Once she listened to her restless agitation, she found that it was driving her to be bold and daring, to do something risky.

Margaret found, as she increased her capacity to tolerate her dread, that she often tried to avoid it by thinking of all the things she had to do for work. When she intensified the feeling she heard herself saying to herself, "I can't handle this work anymore, it's too much." She translated this into a positive action statement: "I won't handle this much work anymore." This pointed her toward giving up many of her projects and decreasing her workload. She realized that she had sacrificed her relationships in order to pursue work-related activities, and she now saw that her restlessness was her feeling that she needed to do something about her romantic life and desire to have children—a message that her personal relationships needed just as much attention as her work life.

9. Once you have a statement of your positive action plan, make a commitment to begin following the directions provided to you. If the action is really scary, you can start small. For example, Margaret realized that it was too threatening for her to call up a man she was attracted to and ask him out for dinner. She decided to start by beginning to accept invitations from other people. As she got comfortable with the dating scene, she figured, she would then take the next step and invite the man she really liked out for coffee. She did not just jump in without thinking; rather, she gradually increased her comfort level with the process of increasing her attention to her romantic life.

10. Take out your journal and review the list of all the activities and internal strategies that you identified in step 3 as tactics for avoiding the feelings of restless agitation. For example, Susan wrote about her compulsion to eat and think constantly about food and diet. Upon reflection, she realized that the time she spent reading diet books, obsessing about what to eat and not to eat, planning how and when she would start her next diet, counting calories, and feeling guilty about eating off-limits foods took up a substantial amount of her time and energy. This list will help you as you read the next section and examine the feeling of worthlessness.

WORTHLESSNESS

One of the most painful and disabling symptoms of depression is the feeling of worthlessness. This can take the form of feeling that you can never do anything right, that you are not loved by anyone, or that there is something fundamentally wrong with you. This symptom may be manifest as an endless rumination about your worth or an ongoing search for some outside source who will tell you that you are worthy.

We will review two ways in which the feelings of worthlessness can be a gift—as a message about how you are spending your time and as an incentive to work toward greater self-acceptance of your limitations. However, the symptom of worthlessness can take on a form that does not offer a gift and can undermine the possibilities of finding the gift in these feelings. We see this form in the person who feels that his essential being is worthless and is preoccupied with finding some external person, panel of judges, or accomplishment that will redeem him from this condition. If you have experienced this form of worthlessness, know that nothing outside of yourself will ever end the search for your worth. In addition, no matter how clear and persuasive an external person may be in his or her proclamation of your worth, if you feel essentially worthless you will find some way to dismiss even the most convincing proclamations.

In David Burns's classic book *Feeling Good: The New Mood Therapy* (1980), he addresses worthlessness and offers a cognitive strategy for challenging it. He suggests that, logically, the concept of "worth" is an abstraction—that it does not exist in any real way. Many people go through life with an imaginary scorecard that measures or counts their units of worth. Getting promoted to the position of manager might earn one a lot of points of worth. Getting fired from a job might subtract almost all the points accumulated to date. This approach to self-worth is fundamentally irrational. Burns suggests that one way to get off this no-win accounting game is simply to assert that every person has one unit of worth and that this cannot be changed by any life events or circumstances. In this way, one gets off the treadmill of constantly seeking more and more points of worth, which never add up to enough.

The Gift of Worthlessness

After proclaiming that your essential worth is not dependent on success or failure, you can begin to search for the meaning of your feelings of worthlessness. One way to understand the gift in these feelings is to translate the feelings into a message about the worthwhileness of how you spend your time.

In declaring that you are a person of essential worth, you have ended the debate about your ultimate value. However, as persons of ultimate worth we are still left with the matter of how we spend our time. There are only so many hours in a day and days in a week. How do the ways in which we spend our time reflect our ultimate worth? For example, Susan, who spent most of her time thinking about food and her weight, found that her feelings of worthlessness were communicating that spending her valuable life essence, time, and energy in constant rumination about her weight was not a worthwhile expenditure of her ultimate worth. She was able to declare to herself that she was worthwhile whether she was fat or thin, whether she ate vegetables or milkshakes. She worked hard to separate her worth from her weight. However, her feelings of worthlessness persisted—clearly, she had not heard the full message in these feelings.

She began to translate these feelings into signals about how she spent her time. She realized that she would rather spend her time creating entertainment that would inspire people while making them laugh. She began to see how her constant rumination about food and her weight interfered with how she really wanted to spend her time. She began to interpret her feelings of worthlessness as a signal to spend her time in the way that was the most meaningful to her: creating entertainment for others. So, every time she felt worthless, instead of thinking about her weight or food she thought about her current projects and what she needed to do to move them forward or get them in front of an audience. In the same way, you can begin to translate your feelings of worthlessness as a signal to engage in more meaningful activities.

EXERCISE: WHAT IS WORTH SPENDING MY ULTIMATE WORTH ON?

1.   Take note the next time you feel worthless. Observe what you do with the feeling and what it makes you think and do. Write your observations in your journal. Susan, for example, noticed that when she felt worthless she would start to plan ways to manage her weight more closely. This often led to obsessive rumination about food and exercise, which, accompanied by harsh words of self-condemnation about her lack of self-control, naturally made her feel worse about herself.

2.   Next time you feel worthless, interpret this feeling as a signal to search for activities that are taking up your time but are not in line with your ultimate worth and therefore are not inherently meaningful. Write a list of your mental or physical activities that are not moving you toward what you really want out of life. The activities Susan wrote down included reading every diet book that came out, calling up her friends to ask for diet advice and exercise tips, and taking exercise classes that she did not enjoy.

3.   After identifying activities that are not worthwhile, ask yourself, "What would I spend my time on if I wasn't wasting it on all these other distractions?" Susan realized she would be putting her ideas down on paper and pitching them to producers. Make a list of all the activities that seem meaningful to you and would move you toward spending your time in ways appropriate to your ultimate worth.

4.   Develop an action plan to reorganize your time so that you spend less time on the worthless activities and more time on the meaningful activities. Write in your journal any positive outcomes that result.

    You may find it easier to identify the nonmeaningful activities than the meaningful ones. If you are having a hard time identifying the most meaningful way to spend your time, the exercise below may help.

EXERCISE: MOVING TOWARD MEANING

It is important to remember that finding the meaning in your life is often like shooting at a moving target. At some stages, professional goals may be the most meaningful activities for you. At other times, devotion to family may carry the highest fulfillment with it. As you develop your gifts, you may hear new messages calling out to find expression in the world. As you can see, finding what is meaningful to you will likely change as you develop and your life challenges evolve. In the following exercise, you will reflect on your desires, with the belief that what you want in your life at the deepest level is guiding you to your area of greatest meaning.

1. If you received a phone call and someone told you the best news you could possibly imagine, who would be calling and what would that person be saying to you? Susan imagined that her call was from her agent, telling her that she had been nominated for an Academy Award. Margaret's imaginary call was from the man of her dreams asking her to go away on a romantic vacation. Your answer to this question will provide you with a sense of the direction you are supposed to be moving in.

2. If you knew for certain that over the next year things in your life were going to get better and better and life would get easier and easier, what would your life look like? What would happen to you and how would you be spending your time?

3. Write down three concrete steps that you could take in the next week that would bring you closer to the life you imagined in step 2. Spend some time planning how you will fit these steps into your schedule, and take action.

INSOMNIA: NOTHING TO LOSE SLEEP OVER

One of the most insidious symptoms of depression is insomnia. You may find yourself unable to go to sleep or waking in the middle of the night unable to go back to sleep. You may be tormented by thoughts that life is meaningless.

The hours you spend tossing and turning in the middle of the night may seem like wasted time, but it can actually be used as a force motivating you to begin the quest for a more meaningful life. Insomnia disrupts your sleep, and you can use the disruptions as a way to find the areas of your life that need to be examined. Insomnia may force you to reflect on your life by giving you distraction-free time to reflect on your life choices and direction. Insomnia can mean "Stop! Wake up! You're about to make a mistake. Think deeply about what you are doing."

Insomnia disrupts not only sleep but also daily life. A person who is fatigued has difficulty functioning during the day. You may find your waking life disrupted after long bouts of insomnia because you can't concentrate or find the energy to complete the life tasks demanded of you. It's commonly said that a person who loses a lot of sleep walks through the day "like a zombie." This evokes the image of a half-alive, half-dead being unthinkingly trudging through life. Or, think of it this way: a person who loses sleep spends at least some of his day in an altered state of consciousness. He may be less sharp and less focused and have difficulty concentrating and making plans.

Sleep deprivation is one of the tactics used to get prisoners of war to confess to crimes, tell military secrets, and reveal other information. This suggests that losing sleep decreases your resistance, makes you lose your judgment, and minimizes your capacity to maintain long-held beliefs and positions. If one gift of depression is that it launches you on the search for meaning, insomnia can play an important role in that search by forcing you to reflect on your current life choices and also shaking up your waking life enough to loosen your perceptions and positions so you can challenge them.

Insomnia Tells You to Wake Up

Insomnia forces you to reflect on your life. When you are awake in the middle of the night there are few distractions. You try to stay in bed, hoping to fall back to sleep, and while you're lying there without anything to do you may find yourself reflecting deeply on your life. The next day, you may spend some of your waking time thinking about a dream you had or an emotion that is bothering you. It may be that you find yourself ruminating about a person or situation and think that that is what is causing you to lose sleep.

It is very important to pay attention to what you are thinking and feeling when you cannot sleep. Usually the content of your thoughts, feelings, or reflections on dreams will provide you with a key to the reason for your depression. The underlying gift of depression at this stage is its ability to orient you to greater meaning. It is a signal that there is a discrepancy between your true desires and your current lifestyle. If this discrepancy between who you are and who you want to be can be called a crisis, the words of Emmy Gut speak to the function of insomnia in reorienting your life. She writes that depression might be an alarm telling us that "all the time and attention we can muster should be devoted to some crisis within ourselves ... depression may signalize that it would be better to engage only in routine activity or even stay at home, to attend to our unattended crisis until we have unraveled what it is about and how it can be remedied. ... The prostrate position very often helps us attend to our inner crisis at last, whereupon we recover" (Gut 1989, p. 14).

Insomnia is telling you to wake up to some conflict in your life that desperately needs your attention. Often, if your days are so tightly scheduled that there is no opportunity for downtime, the only time this message can get through to you is in the middle of the night.

The clues to the substance of the changes that need to be made lie in the feelings and thoughts that trouble you while you are trying to sleep. For example, Jim found his sleep disrupted by thoughts of the woman he was pursuing and her inability to commit to him. He had convinced himself that with enough effort he could win her over. He found now when he could not sleep in the middle of the night that the feelings that kept him awake were those of anger, frustration, and impatience with the woman. He began to realize that there was nothing he could do to change her character and that to continue to pursue her would likely not lead to the commitment he wanted from her. After coming to this realization he broke off his relationship with her and began dating other women. These changes helped relieve his depression.

Insomnia Disrupts Patterns That Are Not Working

There is also a gift in the disruption to your daily life that is caused by insomnia. When insomnia compromises your capacity to function during the day, certain activities and pursuits are the first to fall. A person's whole life does not collapse, but rather certain tasks become more arduous and are the first to suffer. As your level of functioning begins to fall, you can gain hints about the area of your life that is meant to be changed by observing what arena is the first to suffer.

In the example given above, Jim found that his efforts to launch ever greater campaigns to win the heart of the woman he loved were the first to fall. After a sleepless night, his flagging energy and fuzzy state of mind left him to question his efforts, which seemed to yield little of the commitment he hoped to gain. His perception of the failure of these efforts helped him to confirm that this was the area of his life that was off track.

The insomnia was an important communication to help him get back on track and not throw his time and energy into a relationship that he knew, deep down, was not a meaningful one. The following are some questions you can ask yourself that will guide you toward the area in your life that is crying out for deep reflection:

- What personal activities are most disrupted by my loss of sleep?

- What aspects of my life seem not to be impaired by my insomnia?

- Which relationship suffers the most from my inability to function during the day?

- Which professional activities are most impaired by my lack of sleep?

And below are some sentences that you can complete to point you to the area of your life that is asking for reorientation:

- Sometimes in my sleep-deprived, fuzzy state of mind, I begin to question _____ .

- In the middle of the night when I can't sleep I always think about _____ .

- When I'm tossing and turning I feel _____ .

■ The reason I can't sleep is because I keep thinking about

_____ .

■ I could probably fall asleep if it were not for _____ .

These sentences can be used as a guide to point you to the part of your life that is not working and so you can begin making the changes that will put you on the path toward greater meaning in your life.

Chapter 5

Depression as an Inner Revolution

Thoughts of suicide are the most frightening and dangerous symptoms of depression. If you have had suicidal thoughts you were probably frightened by the destructiveness you saw in yourself. Approximately 15 percent of individuals with severe major depression end their lives through suicide, and suicidal thoughts are common in depressed people. However, if you have made serious plans for your suicide, such as thoughts about what sort of a note you would leave or how to leave your affairs in order, then you should recognize these as signs that you urgently need professional help. You should consider an inpatient treatment program until you are certain that you are not a risk to yourself.

If you suffer from suicidal thoughts but know that you would never act on those thoughts, this chapter may help you to find a deeper meaning to your thoughts. The destructiveness of those thoughts is often meant to end an "oppressive regime." One image that can serve you as a guide through the turmoil and darkness is that of the destruction of the Berlin Wall, an imposing structure in Berlin that demarcated the crossing into Communist East Berlin. When the Cold War ended, citizens of that city destroyed the wall. They literally tore the wall down. Their destructiveness symbolized the liberation from the tyranny of oppression.

Similarly, thoughts of suicide may be leading you toward ending oppressive regimes, or making dramatic changes, in your own life. Usually, thoughts of self-destruction indicate an epic struggle to break free from authoritarian rule by someone outside yourself. Suicidal thoughts can lead you toward taking authority for your own life, creating your own rules. The intense pain associated with thoughts and fantasies of ending your own life is caused by unmooring yourself from the familiar drives of your life. Suicidal thoughts and fantasies are telling you that you are about to stage your own personal revolution, one that does not involve harming yourself. You are always in control of yourself. Sometimes committing suicide seems like a way to avoid making major life changes. But remember that in reality any life change—no matter how dramatic—will always be easier to make than committing suicide.

While suicidal thoughts are the extreme form of an inner revolution, many related symptoms of depression can be seen as an effort to get you to reflect deeply on the need for dramatic changes in your life. This chapter will show you how to make those changes in gentle ways and help you resolve the symptoms of depression.

BEING NOBODY, GOING NOWHERE

The revolution you are about to undergo usually means the overthrow of two things in your life: (1) other people's authority and (2) the tyranny of doing. Thoughts of self-destruction mean that you are trying to "kill off" parts of yourself that have been directed by other people (Rosen 2002). In addition, thoughts of ending your life can lead to freedom from the compulsion to always be doing something important. Many times when people come to the brink of death they realize that their intense suffering was caused by their need to do something with their life. A vivid fantasy of death may be a grim force that gives you the permission to just be. For some, only the thought of death frees them to live a life of "being nobody going nowhere" (Khema 2001).

In your day-to-day life, if you buy into the culture's demands that you do, achieve, and constantly grow, then the prospect of allowing yourself to just *be* can seem like the end of the world. What would it be like to be a nobody? To go nowhere? To do nothing? To many of us it really seems like a pointless existence—or a death. The gift of being "a nobody going nowhere" is that it liberates us to just be. Liberation is what is behind those destructive thoughts and fantasies of ending your own life: the liberation into being.

The pressure to perform makes it difficult for most of us to even imagine the value of being over doing. My own revelation that allowed me to explore this quality in my life began with a series of dreams. The first dream centered on a bunch of people sitting on a stoop, drinking lemonade and watching people walk by. In considering this dream I kept asking myself, "But what are they doing?" Over and over I asked myself this question, trying to get to the bottom of it. Finally, with the force of an epiphany I realized, "They are not doing anything!" That was the point of the dream—people doing nothing. It was hard to imagine.

Peter C. Whybrow (2005), author of *American Mania: When More Is Not Enough*, has argued that our cultural pressure to get bigger, faster, and stronger is making individuals sick, either bringing on depression or health problems caused by exhaustion. The cultural preference for doing instead of being can be seen in how easily we diagnose and medicate children, who are naturally gurus when it comes to just being. If a child seems to daydream or follow his or her impulses too much, the adults in that child's life may be tempted to give the child medication in order to make him or her meet expectations in school (Honos-Webb 2005a). For adults, the pressure to do and perform is even more intense. When this cultural pressure becomes internalized, suicidal impulses can emerge as an urge to kill off the oppressive, never-ending demand for improved performance, achievement, and expansion. Depression itself can be seen as a rebellion against the persistent and pervasive insistence to do more, to move faster, to compete and win.

INNER REVOLUTION

As we've discussed, the urge to take your own life can actually be the impulse to overthrow a harsh expectation or unrealistic demand that you have imposed on yourself. The gift of suicidal thoughts is that they can be translated into the impulse to achieve freedom from inner tyranny.

Some common experiences of such a revolution involve changing from doing to being, from living for the future to living in the now, and from living from a "must" to living from a "may." In each of these revolutions, beliefs and expectations about yourself that are unrealistic, harsh, and rigid are overthrown.

Unrealistic, Harsh, and Rigid Beliefs

What do I mean by "unrealistic"? This is something that requires more energy, skills, talents, and time than you have available in order to achieve it. For example, if you expect to be liked by everyone in your personal and professional life, then you have set an expectation that neither you nor anyone else could ever achieve. Many mothers labor to fulfill unrealistic expectations, thinking that they must give their children every advantage. But no mother has the time, energy, or skills to run her children to every conceivable brain-building activity while offering perfect doses of discipline balanced with unconditional love. Another unrealistic goal may be one that is not in alignment with your own greatest gifts and talents. A person who wants to be an actor because of the attendant fame and glory but doesn't really have the natural skills or talents necessary for the craft would benefit from redirection away from such an unrealistic pursuit.

A harsh belief or expectation is one that leads you to beat yourself up in different ways when you fall short of your goals. For example, a person who has a harsh belief that she must be successful might drive herself into the ground working around the clock. When she falls short, she may call herself harsh names, telling herself that she is not worth anything. In short, a person becomes emotionally abusive toward herself when her self-expectations are harsh.

A rigid belief or expectation is one that is very specific but does not incorporate any flexibility regarding how to satisfy the expectation. One woman insisted that in the next year she had to meet and marry a man who was well educated, financially secure, attractive, and emotionally sensitive. When she failed to meet this rigid expectation, she began to experience suicidal thoughts. She realized that she might have an easier time meeting her need to have an intimate relationship if she were more flexible about what she needed in order to feel satisfied.

Unrealistic, harsh, and rigid expectations can lead to tragedy. One young man, who had been straight-A student in high school, started to slack off in college and began to fail. He fell into a severe depression and committed suicide. The unrealistic and rigid expectations held by him and his parents had led him to believe that if he was not a good student then he was a complete failure and would not have any future. It is heartbreaking to think that his life could have been saved if he had gained insight into the narrowness of his view about his own personal worth and identity.

FOUR PRINCIPLES OF CHANGE

If you are experiencing suicidal thoughts, then this may be a sign that some areas of yourself are beginning to revolt under the weight of too many unrealistic beliefs. What parts of yourself are staging the coup? For each person it may be different, but there are four common struggles, or urges, that you may identify with. Urges (you might also call them "struggles" or "needs") are the parts of yourself that don't fit into your rigid, harsh, and unrealistic demands. Four urges that are seeking expression are (1) the permission principle, (2) the pleasure principle, (3) the presence principle, and (4) the power principle.

These four principles represent a "cheat sheet" of needs for you to experiment with. By giving expression to these four needs, you will advance on the path of self-transformation, which those suicidal thoughts and feelings may be pushing you toward. Marianne Williamson has written the following about the impulse toward change: "This is the time of a Great Beginning. It is time to die to who we used to be and to become instead who we are capable of being. That is the gift that awaits us now: the chance to become who we really are" (2005, p. 12). Depression can be your effort to make drastic life changes by getting rid of belief systems that interfere with your ability to be your true self.

The exercises below are intended to help you cope with suicidal thoughts and feelings. They will also help you cope with constant self-judgment if you are tyrannized by harsh, unrealistic, and rigid beliefs. These exercises are meant to help you translate these thoughts into a gift. *If you have any intention or plan to act on your self-destructive thoughts or feelings, then you must seek professional help immediately.*

The Permission Principle

Many people who are depressed punish themselves relentlessly, increasing the severity of their depression. One way to turn this around is to practice giving yourself permission. The following exercise will help you identify key areas in which you are restricting yourself unnecessarily.

EXERCISE: GIVING YOURSELF PERMISSION

1. This first step isn't going to make any sense to you. Don't worry about that. Sometimes nonsense can help you get beyond your rational mind in order to learn things about yourself that are just below conscious awareness. So suspend your rational mind for a moment and get out your journal. Write the following ten times: "If I were not alive I would be able to _____." Now, write ten responses to complete the sentence. Don't put too much thought into the answers—just write what comes into your head.

2. Review your responses and circle the ones that are the most interesting to you. What have you stopped yourself from doing or being? For example, Georgette, a chiropractor who had spent many years and a great deal of money to obtain her degree and training, was surprised at her responses. She found that the answer that resonated most was that she could stop being a chiropractor. She had gone to school because she loved to heal bodies, but her job was physically demanding, and she had begun to believe that her patients' underlying psychological issues were at the root of the health problems she was treating with physical manipulations. Yet she had continued in her practice because she believed that she had invested too much time and money to be able to quit.

3. Now, in your journal, write the following question: "What do I need so much that I am willing to die for it?" In answering this question, write freely without censoring yourself. Georgette found herself writing that she needed to pursue her interest in psychological healing of physical problems, an interest that she had not explored because of her investment in her chiropractic career.

4. Next, write the following in your journal: "It is difficult for me to give myself permission to _____ because _____ ." Complete this sentence. Georgette wrote that it was difficult for her to give herself permission to pursue her new interest because she worried her mother would say she was flaky and that her new interest was just as fleeting as her previous interest in being a chiropractor.

5. Ask yourself: "Whose judgment am I most worried about?" After you have come up with an answer, ask yourself, "Is it worth it to sacrifice my inner life because of what another person or group of people think about me?" Georgette's response was that she was worried that her family and clients would think she was not serious because she kept changing her interests. Although she didn't like the idea of changing her course because of the money she owed in student loans, the force of her suicidal thoughts made her realize that her life was more important than her financial status.

6. In your journal, write the following at the top of each of five consecutive pages: "I give myself permission to . . ." Then, without editing yourself, write a different response to that stem on each of the five pages. Review what you have written and consider what changes you can make that would allow you to give yourself more permission. Keep track of how this affects your depression and thoughts of suicide. Georgette, for example, found that by giving herself permission to pursue her new interest and put her passion ahead of her financial standing, her interest in life was renewed and she no longer thought about killing herself.

The Pleasure Principle

Depression often maintains itself through a rigid form of self-denial. The simple act of seeking pleasure can turn things around for you.

EXERCISE: FINDING YOUR PLEASURE

In this exercise you will be asked to spend some time living based on the pleasure principle, doing what feels good. It is your natural birth-right to experience pleasure and to learn your life lessons through pleasure. It really is possible and reasonable to learn important life lessons, pay your dues, build character, and give yourself a badge of honor through pleasure. The oppressive regime that your depression is trying to overthrow may be the belief that you must suffer in order to learn and grow.

The first part of this exercise will help you connect to your bodily sense of pleasure. Have you ever been in an interview or other formal situation in which you remained in an uncomfortable physical position so as not to appear too fidgety or to avoid calling attention to yourself? This can be a metaphor for how some people live their whole lives: restraining their natural impulses toward pleasure so as not to disturb others. This is the opposite of the pleasure principle. Your physical body has a sense of what is comfortable and pleasurable. The pleasure principle generally drives your body to move, to be active, to rest, and to be still at times. Your goal for this exercise is to get in sync with your body's need for pleasure.

1. Give yourself fifteen minutes in a place where you will not be distracted or interrupted. Take a few deep breaths and focus on your body. Use your attention to do a full body scan. To do a body scan turn your mental attention to your head and notice any physical sensations there. Observe without judging any feel-ings, and continue to do so over the rest of your body. Bring your attention back to the sensations in your body if you find your mind wandering. The practice of doing regular body scans is one component toward increasing your body mindfulness (Marra 2005).

   Your goal is to find your body's impulse. What does your body want to do? How does it want to move? Move your body in whatever way feels good. Maybe you want to stretch. Maybe you're tired and want to lie down. Maybe you are hyper and want to jump around. Let your body lead and do whatever it feels like doing. Do not hold back if your body changes its tempo. Maybe at one minute your movements are flowing and soft and the next minute your movements are harsh and abrupt. This will let you practice increasing your awareness of what feels pleasurable and following that pleasure.

2.   The next part of the exercise is simply to increase your awareness of how you currently relate to your need for pleasure. For one day, make a point of observing how often you feel pleasure, how often you restrain it, and how often you let it guide your life. It can be as simple as what you listen to in the car on the way to work. Do you listen to educational tapes in order to use the time productively when you would rather listen to pop music? Do you listen to your children's music in order to keep them happy when you would rather listen to talk radio? Or it could be as significant as the job you go to. Just observe what your pleasure is and what you actually do and why. You don't have to make any changes; just notice. You may find it helpful to write your observations down in your journal.

3.   After increasing your awareness of the role pleasure plays in your life, you will want to practice making a few changes in your life to let your pleasure guide you. Start with the small things. Maybe you'll decide to light candles and use your expensive china when eating breakfast. Maybe you will choose to listen to pop songs on the radio rather than French language tapes. Make a small change and notice how that feels. Keep a record of the small changes you make that increase your pleasure. On days when you feel helpless, you can return to the list for ideas on how to change your mood.

CRAVINGS

One thing you should be aware of is the difference between being guided by your pleasure and giving into a compulsive craving. For example, for a recovering alcoholic it would be a mistake to give in to the compulsive craving for a drink, even though that drink might bring them temporary pleasure.

If you have a compulsive craving, you can still let it guide you in the following way. Ask yourself, "What is the state or feeling that my compulsive craving gives me?" Your answer will tell you what feeling you need more of in your life. If you respond, "A glass of wine would give me a feeling of being relaxed and not worrying about everything," then give yourself permission to relax and not worry. Set aside some time for not worrying. If you are afraid that your life will fall apart if you stop worrying, you can remind yourself that you are allowed to start worrying when that time period has come to an end.

If you are depressed, these exercises will predictably stir up an impulse to punish yourself. You will want to honor and give voice to that part of yourself. The self-punishment is actually a misguided attempt at protecting you—it is trying to remind you about the misguided "no pain, no gain" belief you may have internalized. You will need to bring this voice into awareness and allow it expression so you can soften the voice. Once you allow this voice to express itself, you can expect some lessening of your harsh self-judgments or thoughts about committing suicide.

EXERCISE: MAKING SPACE FOR YOUR PUNISHING VOICE

1. When you are working on allowing yourself to be guided by pleasure, pay attention and listen for the voice of punishment. In your journal, write about what this harsh voice sounds like. Does it tell you that you will fail if you feel pleasure? Does it tell you that feeling pleasure will turn you into your ne'er-do-well parent, sibling, or friend? Give this voice expression. Write what it has to say to you.

2. Once you have given your voice of punishment a chance to express itself, ask the voice the following question: "What are you trying to protect me from?" Write whatever comes into your mind. If you can't think of a single answer, write this question ten times and each time write whatever comes into your mind.

3. Now you can begin a dialogue with this voice. You might reassure it that its fears are not reasonable. Perhaps you can find a way to achieve what the voice wants in other ways. Jenine found that the voice was telling her that if she let her pleasure guide her, she would become obese like her twin sister. In writing out a

dialogue between the punishing voice and the pleasure-seeking part of her, she was able to create a plan that involved seeking pleasure by being involved in group sports. This calmed her fears that experiencing pleasure would cause her to eat nonstop and become obese.

The point of the above exercise is to transform the voice of self-punishment into a voice of self-care. In Jenine's case, the harsh voice that wouldn't allow her to connect with her own pleasure and let it guide her was transformed into a caring voice that said, "Be careful. I'm concerned that you might lose control and become like your sister."

The Presence Principle

You may have found that your suicidal impulses or punitive judgments often follow a failure to achieve something or an ending of a relationship. Your suicidal thoughts and fantasies can be translated into an attempt to free yourself from the compulsion to do and achieve. The presence principle is that part of yourself that wants to just be, and to enjoy life. The presence principle is that part of yourself that understands that who you are is not dependent on what you do, what you have, or how impressive your accomplishments are.

When my children were born, I said to each one, "You don't have to be anything or do anything. We just brought you here to show you how much we love you." The pain of your depression may force you to learn to mother and nurture yourself in this way. If you can diminish the dominance of the need to prove yourself, you'll gain access to the part of yourself that showers you with love for just being. You can be like the characters in the dream I described at the beginning of the chapter, who just sat on a stoop doing nothing—just being and enjoying. This exercise will help you connect with this part of yourself.

Of course, you do not want to completely eliminate the part of yourself that lives in the past, plans for the future, and delights in achievement. Planning, doing, and achieving should be central in your life—it's just that your sense of worthiness should be liberated from these activities. Thomas Marra (2005) advises keeping a balance between being present in the moment and paying attention to long-term goals.

EXERCISE: JUST BE IT

While there are many disciplines, techniques, and technologies that are intended to help people be present in the now, these strategies involve effortful struggle toward just being and therefore paradoxically undermine just being. Using the violent destruction of the Berlin Wall as an emblem of the liberation, freedom is achieved by tearing down oppressive structures rather than through seeking the state itself. We usually understand freedom to be freedom from something. In the case of depression it is typically freedom from rigid, unrealistic, and harsh expectations. Therefore, a sense of presence is achieved by taking down barriers around it, as the following exercise will show you.

Remember that these exercises are intended to help you cope with suicidal thoughts and feelings. If you have any intention or plan to act on these thoughts or feelings, you must seek professional help immediately. These exercises are meant to help you translate your self-punishing thoughts into a gift, but only once you are certain that you are safe from actually harming yourself.

1. Monitor yourself so you become aware when a harsh judgment or fantasy of ending your life comes into your mind. Observe your reaction to the suicidal or destructive impulse. Do you become afraid? Do you become angry? Do you become sad? Whatever reaction you have, observe it and record it in your journal. Do any visual images enter into your mind after a bout with these harsh, punishing thoughts? Write free associations about the images that come into your mind for as long as you can.

2. When you feel a punitive emotion or think a suicidal thought, you can practice translating the destructive fantasy into a force for personal transformation. Think about the destruction of the Berlin Wall: this image can serve as a guide for how to channel your internal violent messages toward your own liberation from harsh,

unreasonable, and rigid demands on yourself. To help you figure out what needs to be torn down, fill in the blanks in the following sentences:

- If I died, I would not have to do _____ .

- If I died, I would not have to achieve _____ .

- If I died, I wouldn't feel like a failure for _____ .

- If I died, I wouldn't have to blame myself for _____ .

- If I died, I wouldn't have to work so hard to _____ .

- If I died, I wouldn't have to compete with _____ .

- If I died, I wouldn't have to take care of _____ .

- If I died, I wouldn't worry about solving _____ 's problems.

- If I died, I could let go of the need to _____ .

- If I died, I would be free of _____ .

3. Review the above completed sentences, which will probably give you an idea of how to tranlate your suicidal thoughts and feelings into an urge to liberate yourself. What do you want to free yourself from? Write your response in your journal.

4. Imagine that you could have a surgery that would completely remove the oppressive demands that you have identified. What would your life be like and what would you feel like? Write as much as possible about the details of your new life.

5. Many people with depression find that without the achievements and accomplishments they demand of themselves they feel insecure or worthless. Make a list of the activities you pursue just to prove your worth.

6. Once you become aware of which activities you are doing for the purpose of increasing your self-worth, you can begin to examine

whether spending your energy to prove your worth is reasonable to you. Ask yourself the following questions:

- Whose approval do I need in order to feel worthy?

- What does this person need to say to me so I feel worthy?

- What do I need to do in order to feel worthy myself?

- How much is enough to make me believe I have achieved my ultimate worth?

- What will be the signal to me that I have finally achieved my ultimate worth?

- What will happen if I never grasp that golden ring of achievement that will lead me to earn my ultimate worth?

- If a panel of judges were assembled to determine my worth or lack of worth, who would be on that panel, and why?

- Do I really want to give those people the power to determine my worth?

After completing the above exercise you will begin to see that working to earn your worth is really related to issues of power. You have the power to give your ultimate worth to yourself.

The Power Principle

One of the possible gifts of depression is the transformation that allows you to become the dominant authority in your own life. You get to take control and determine whose opinions are important to you and in what circumstances. You get to take over and create a life that is in alignment with your deepest desires, values, and talents.

The main threat to feeling your power and being guided by it is the belief that you are a victim. Perhaps you have been victimized in the past and have generalized that experience to the rest of your life.

Perhaps you never made the developmental transition to independent adulthood and still feel dependent on others for your survival. Or perhaps for a long time you have simply let others make difficult life decisions for you.

Even if you have felt like a victim and don't feel your own power yet, depression is a signal that you are beginning the process of taking control of your own life. Let's look at Katy's experience to see how depression can signify a change in the works.

■ Katy's Story

Katy's husband left her shortly after their son was diagnosed with autism. She raged against him and his heartlessness for abandoning her during the most difficult time of her life. She stewed in her anger at him for ruining her life. Her depression got so intense that she began having suicidal thoughts. After some reflection, she realized that she felt suicidal every time she was faced with a major decision about her son's care. She felt that she wasn't capable of making complex decisions without her husband, who had always told her that she was stupid and couldn't think very clearly.

However, she knew she had no choice but to take the chance of making a mistake. As she began to organize a treatment plan for her son and weigh all of the options, she realized that she was quite good at finding new resources and getting her son what he needed. As she watched her son make many improvements, she gained confidence in her own abilities to think clearly and make complicated decisions. She realized that she didn't need her husband and his constant insults. She began to reclaim her intellectual skills and talents.

Not only could she survive without her husband—she could also thrive. She began to stop feeling sorry for herself because her husband left her. She came to see that had he stayed he would have actually interfered with her son getting the treatment he needed, because he never fully accepted the reality of their son's situation. She stopped feeling like a victim and she stopped feeling like she couldn't take care of herself. She began thinking of herself as very capable and competent. She gained a sense of her power and promise.

EXERCISE: EVERYTHING YOU EVER WANTED

The following exercise will give you a sample of reclaiming your power to author your own life and opinions of yourself.

1. Imagine you are sitting in your home and you hear a knock at the door. Who, in your heart of hearts, do you hope it will be when you open the door?

2. Imagine that you open the door and standing there is the very person you secretly hoped to see. Imagine that this person comes in and you have a long and soulful conversation. What does this person say to you? What is the most empowering message you could hear from this person? Write this down in your journal.

3. Whatever the message is, give yourself the power to declare that it is true for you. Give yourself permission to send this empowering message to yourself as many times as you need to throughout the day. You might want to write it down on a card and carry it in your purse or wallet so you can read it whenever you get a chance, or you might want to make a poster emblazoned with this message and hang it in your home. Allow yourself to get creative and use computer graphics, photos cut from magazines, paints, crayons, or whatever is appealing to you. Post your message wherever you can. Say it to yourself at every opportunity. You can even make an audio recording of it and play it back as often as possible.

4. Once you empower yourself, you may find that the voice of the victim becomes stronger as you begin to give yourself authority. Like any oppressive regime, your experience of being a victim has a stake in maintaining its place in your inner world. You may feel fear at losing the voice of the victim because it has become so familiar to you. It is important to give the victim voice expression and to honor it. Ask that voice, "What are you trying to do for me?" Write your response in your journal.

5. The voice of the victim within you is most likely trying to protect you from being taken advantage of or hurt. Look at your response to the question in step 4, and ask yourself, "How can I achieve this aim (i.e., protect myself) without feeling like a victim?"

Try writing a dialogue between these two parts of yourself—the victim and the newfound powerful authority. You will become more powerful and capable of protecting yourself.

In this chapter, we have seen that even the most dangerous and frightening symptoms of depression may have a gift to offer you: they may be sending an urgent message to "kill off" rigid, harsh, and unreasonable demands that threaten your freedom to live in alignment with your highest ideals and desires. By listening to these thoughts, you can translate them into tools to help you live with permission, pleasure, presence, and power. However, as we've discussed, it is of utmost importance that you seek professional help if you think that suicidal or self-punishing thoughts may pose a threat to your own safety.

Chapter 6

Depression as a Way of Reclaiming Grief

Loss is fundamental to the human predicament. It is not something we can control, prevent, or change. We can, however, control how we relate to loss. And how we relate to loss will determine how we live our lives. The point of this chapter is not that loss is a gift—it may or may not be a gift, depending on the situation. But choosing to grieve a loss will yield many gifts for you, and primary among these gifts is connecting you more deeply to your heart.

Grieving losses involves dwelling on that which was lost—the person, the part of yourself, the time of your life—and turning events into experiences. Grieving is a dwelling, a reworking, a revisiting. Grieving is forming a relationship with loss itself and reforming a relationship with who or what was lost. Grieving involves re-membering—making what was lost a member of your inner world in a different way.

Maybe it was a family member who died. Maybe it was a husband whom you've divorced. Maybe it was the single life you left when you married. Maybe it was a life of independence you lost when you had children. Maybe it was a city you left when you moved to a new home. Each of these losses needs to be absorbed and processed to make meaning of the loss so you can find the gift in the relationship.

If you try to race past a loss without relating to it in a profound and deep way, it is likely that depression will result. Grief is a natural and predictable result of loss, and ignoring its power can result in depression, substance abuse, and other mental health afflictions. Depression offers a gift to you in teaching you how to relate to loss.

DEPRESSION SAYS "SLOW DOWN"

When you are hit with a depression after a loss, you lose interest in your daily activities. Your blue mood slows you down and makes you dwell on the loss. Poor concentration impairs your efforts to return to normal. These symptoms are telling you that there is no normal to go back to. The loss is meant to change you. Depression gives you the opportunity to learn a new way of relating to the inevitable losses of life. As psychologist James Hillman has written, "soul slows the parade of history; digestion tames appetite; experience coagulates events. I believe that had we more experiencing there would be need for fewer events and the quick passage of time would find a stop. . . . What we do not digest is laid out somewhere else, into others, the political world, the dreams, the body's symptoms, becoming literal and outer . . . because it is too hard for us, too opaque, to break open and to insight" (1983, p. 27).

What Hillman is alluding to is that if you do not "digest" your losses, you may find your life becomes increasingly meaningless. Rather than being present for your life, you will feel that it is just passing you by. If you cannot relate to your losses, your capacity to relate to others in meaningful ways is impaired.

Until you feel your loss and realize that you can still live in the face of irrevocable loss, your relationships will be haunted by the fear that if you get too close, you will experience another loss. When you realize that you can survive a deeply felt loss, you can connect deeply without a fear that holds you back. Depression gives you the gift of slowing you down so you can be free to connect deeply with others.

A MORE INTENSE PRESENCE

There comes a time in the process of grief when grieving no longer means dwelling on the emptiness of loss. After a period of grieving and honoring the stages of grief, the emptiness of loss becomes an opening into the fullness of all that was and in some mystical sense still is. The stages between feeling the emptiness and the fullness of loss can take months, years, or decades, depending on the individual. But the time spent grieving is not wasted. Grieving is like polishing rare stones and jewels. The process of going over and over the memories creates a rare and beautiful jewel, the true beauty of which had not been previously realized. There are lessons here for the life you are living now.

Part of grieving is reflecting on what seemed like ordinary moments and realizing how essentially meaningful those moments were. Whether they are memories of simple meals shared or singing silly songs together, in the face of loss you realize that these were among the most significant moments of your life.

These realizations can affect your current day-to-day life. Each encounter in your present life can now be seen as a diamond in the rough. You no longer need to wait until the tragedy of loss occurs to see the intensity and light of the present moment. After many rounds of intense grieving, you may see that previously mundane, unremarkable moments can become transformed into events of momentous splendor. You may become determined not to miss such momentous events in the present unfolding of your life. Grieving trains you to liberate the splendor possible in each moment.

With this training and knowledge, you will be able to bring that intense presence into your current relationships.

A Gift of Depression: Connecting to Your Heart

Depression stops you in your tracks and reminds you to reflect on your losses even when the rest of the world tells you to move on. When your heart is breaking because of a tragic loss, the demands of the real world fall away. You become attuned to every nuance of your feelings and memories that play through your mind. Because you suddenly see the triviality of everything except for the enormity of the loss you are facing, you gain an enormous power to concentrate on the subtle energies in your heart.

This highly attuned state increases your sensitivity to yourself and to others. You gain much compassion for yourself and for others. When others go through loss you will be able to recognize the agony and reach out in support because you will have gone through hell and been able to return to tell your story.

This development of the intelligence of the heart is an organic outcome of grief. There are spiritual disciplines and psychological practices designed to help people achieve similar goals. Doc Childre (Childre and Rozman 2003), who developed the HeartMath method of increasing the intelligence of the heart, has written the following wisdom:

> What your heart tells you at any time matches your readiness to hear it. Your heart intuition unfolds as you grow in emotional maturity. As you increase your ratio of being "in the heart" versus being "in the head," you'll find new insights for dealing with triggers and releasing emotional histories. You will get to the point where you recognize when you are reacting from your old "head" self, then choose to go to your heart to find your real self. (p. 51)

The last chapter revealed the ways in which depression can be a message to overthrow the dominance of your "head," which manifested itself in the form of harsh, unrealistic, and rigid beliefs. Childre and Rozman (2003) describe a specific technique for facilitating the emotional maturity of leading with your heart:

> The Heart Lock-In technique is designed to help you generate and sustain coherence and distinguish between your head voice and your heart voice. To sustain emotional coherence, you focus your attention in the area of your heart and learn to send positive feelings out to others or to yourself. If emotional histories and reactions come up while you do this, you send them love. When thoughts pull you into the head, you bring your focus back to the heart. You keep pulling your energy from the head back down to the heart and build power to stay in your heart. It's nature's design that you get your head in sync with your deeper heart intent. (p. 51)

This specific technique bears many similarities to the process of grieving. Grieving usually involves fond memories of appreciation for the person who is gone or the lifestyle you have left: emotional histories and reactions often come up. This technique both mirrors the process of grief and offers guidance for how to be transformed by grief. Their suggestion is to stay in the heart when the drama of the loss itself comes up. By following their technique you can accelerate your potential to grow from your grief rather than be destroyed by it. Since your depression may be a message to you to listen to your grief, once you hear the message your depression no longer serves any purpose and will likely resolve itself.

YOU BECOME MORE LOVING

A heartbreak denied leads to death in life. Your heart will harden if you attempt to stave off the pain you know is there. In contrast, if you go to the ends of your own heartaches, you will carve out depths that contain vast amounts of loving energy. The pain etches deep valleys in your heart, and these valleys measure the span of your ability to love. Having weathered a loss you will reach your own deepest capacity for loving others.

Our current culture's promotion of chronic self-improvement as the path to finding love and healing may have it all wrong. It may be that you don't find love by becoming a shinier, happier person. You find love not by becoming more lovable but ultimately by becoming more loving. You do this by honoring every movement of your heart, and that means facing the ache of loss. We can thank depression for making this possible. We would probably never choose to face these losses if depression didn't stop us in our tracks and force us to focus on what's most important.

YOU BECOME MORE INTUITIVE

In order to make your way through our increasingly complex world you will need to rely more and more on intuition. There are too many choices these days, too many possible outcomes. Your intuition can lead you out of the confusing maze in a way that rational analysis cannot.

Intuition comes from deep connection to the energies of your heart. Even if—especially if—the heart is in pain, tuning into its energies connects you with an intelligence far more vast and subtle than that of your head. Belleruth Naparstek, in writing about opening up to one's sixth sense, said that "when people can allow themselves to experience the full impact of their pain, without numbing it or shutting it down, they generate a lot of energy around their hearts, and this can spring them wide open. . . . One healer told me how the heartbreak of getting out of her second marriage was a major force that propelled further opening in her" (1997, p. 47).

The power of connecting deeply with this most human pain of loss is that it increases your capacity to read others' feelings and impressions on a subtle level.

A Gift of Depression: Becoming Your Own Source

When faced with irrevocable loss you may be transformed by the sheer force of your intense longing for reconnection with the person or thing you lost, as that longing collides with the sheer impossibility of fulfill-ment. It takes a great deal of inner space to let this process happen. Depression clears out the distractions of your normal life to give you the space to do this work.

The powerful longing you experience will ignite your imagination as you create mental scenes of reunions or of life as it might be if the loss had never occurred. If you allow yourself to remain present for the tension between your desires and the impossibility of having them met, you may have a revelation, recognizing that you can meet your own needs. If you lose a mother, you learn you can mother yourself. If you lose a lover, you learn you can love yourself.

As you sit in your longing, you will ultimately abandon the quest for its fulfillment in the outer world. You will have become the source of fulfillment.

A Gift of Depression: Singularity

While grieving the loss of a person in your life, you may find yourself grieving the loss of parts of yourself that you have outgrown. Again, depression forces you to slow down and reflect on who you have become, and how you have been shaped by forces that are no longer important to you.

As you grieve outworn aspects of your identity you may feel lonely more often than before. One gift of grief is singularity: you become more yourself, which necessarily means that you become more different from others. This happens because the parts of yourself that you let go of in depression are usually conformity to others' expectations and the compulsive need for approval, both of which make it easier for you to get along and blend in with others. We have primal instincts that make us fear standing out on our own; becoming your own authority is scary work. But facing your fears gives you the opportunity to become a hero to yourself. As Lamya Surya Das writes, "All heroes have at least one quality in common: They don't run away from their fears. Heroes are just as afraid as the rest of us, but they have learned how to confront and walk through their terrors. Quite simply, heroes aren't afraid of being afraid" (Das 2003, p. 123).

Your singularity and originality is the expression of your most essential self. If you cut off your heartaches you are cutting off a substantial part of your emotional self and the sensitivity, energy, and intelligence that is yours alone. Belleruth Naparstek writes, "Even the more uncomfortable feelings, such as pain, grief, envy, shame, and fury, are a vast energy source, a furnace full of powerful psychic fuel. We would no more want to disconnect from our feelings than we would want to be unplugged from our vital life force" (1997, p. 49).

The grief of loss pushes you outside of your normal state of consciousness, and you become deranged in some small way. We have always known that there is some connection between madness and genius. Heartbreak pushes you close to the edge of sanity without having to fully lose it. Depression stops you from rushing past your heartbreak and pretending you don't care; in this way it helps you to maintain your originality and uniqueness.

A Gift of Grief: Communality

Paradoxically, while grief allows you to become more singular, at the same time it increases your capacity to feel interdependent and connected with others. Everyone experiences tragic losses. The deeper you can enter into your loss, the more connected you will be with everyone else. By listening to your depression, which pulls you out of your daily activities so that you can dwell in your emotional response to your losses, you will gain access to some of the most fundamental human experiences shared by everyone.

If you try to steel yourself against the pain of loss, you will feel increasingly lonely, alienated, and isolated. You may feel that your loss is unique and that no one could ever understand the nature of your loss. You are right. But everyone else will have losses that are similarly singular in their pain and impact. So, while the particular nature and pain of your loss is unique, the fact of your pain and loss is not.

Grief then becomes your bridge that allows you to connect with others. The deeper you go into your own grief, the more you can share with others who have lost. In this way, depression, by slowing you down and forcing you to relate to your loss, is forging your link to others.

In one mystical tradition a guru taught his students that the pain of life is like salt. If you dissolve the salt in a glass of water, he said, the water will not taste good. If you dissolve the same amount of salt in a lake, the salt will not be noticeable. "Don't be a glass—become a lake," the guru advised. By connecting with your own grief, you can connect with others' grief and forge bonds of communality.

A Gift of Depression: Vulnerability

Grief makes you aware of your own vulnerability. When you lose someone close to you, you recognize your own mortality. When someone leaves you, you realize that you can drive people away. When you let go of a central and familiar part of your identity, you see that who you are is not as stable and permanent as you might have wished. A dream that never came true may cause you to recognize your limitations.

As you experience your vulnerability, you may begin to feel weak and fragile. This feeling of fragility may feel new to you. As you expand to allow more of this feeling, you may feel a strange sense of opening to movement and energy. In this state of fragility, you openly face the shards of your broken dreams and hopes. Your openness to this experience may allow you the fluidity to pick up the broken shards and arrange them in a pattern, like a mosaic or a stained glass window. You can become capable of creating something hauntingly beautiful and strangely original from this colorful collection of broken shards.

Vulnerability of the heart is a natural outcome of grief. The work of Doc Childre demonstrates that emotional maturity is associated with this quality. He writes, "Heart vulnerability is listening to what your heart wants, without the mind filtering the heart's message to get what the mind wants. Responding from the head and not staying open in the heart is one of the biggest causes of emotional pain and regret" (Childre and Martin 1999, p. 86).

When depression forces you to slow down and forge a relationship with loss, it offers you a gift: a chance to develop the strength, sensitivity, and intelligence of your heart, through vulnerability.

In his book *Soul Prints*, Marc Gafni points to the movie *Rocky* to illustrate the power of vulnerability:

> At the movie's great turning point, Rocky cries out from the depths of his being, "Aaaadrieeenne!" He is saying, "Adrienne, I need you! I can't do it without you!" At that moment, a new sort of power and perfection surges through Rocky. Immediately following we see a transformed Rocky, running, triumphant—and we hear his special music. He has acknowledged need, and he has become more whole. (2001, p. 107)

Just identifying your vulnerability will help you honor the gift in your depression and recover. Grief helps you to recognize your dependence on others and gain clarity about the depth and focus of your own needs.

FROM HEAD TO HEART

Like any major transition in your life, even the change toward opening your heart will require you to grieve the loss of a previous lifestyle. In the exercise below you will practice grieving the departure of a part of yourself—a life dominated by your head.

Many books have been written about grieving, including *Grieving Mindfully* by Sameet Kumar (2005), *Grief's Courageous Journey* by Caplan and Lang (1995), and *Surviving the Death of Your Spouse* by Deborah Levinson (2004). These books provide many resources and exercises for facilitating the grieving process.

An important part of this process involves re-membering lost loved ones into your inner world. This means to incorporate the person permanently in some meaningful way as a member of your community.

In the case of death, this may take the form of rituals, such as honoring the person's memory by lighting a candle on important anniversaries. It may take the form of creating memorials or hanging beloved photos in prominent places. In the case of divorce, it may take the form of honoring the gifts in your life that would not be there had this person not been a part of your life.

We are accustomed to the idea of grieving the loss of people we loved, but grieving the loss of a part of oneself or one's life is equally important. The failure to grieve the loss of a part of yourself or a change of lifestyle can lead you to get stuck and fail to make the necessary developmental leap to the next part of your life. Everyone knows someone who has failed to grow up in some way, like the married man who thinks it's appropriate to ogle other women even when his wife is present. He has failed to grieve his days as a single guy.

I remember being surprised after the birth of my first child that, in addition to the jaw-dropping awe and heart-exploding love I felt toward this miracle of life, I continued to have memories of the carefree and footloose times I had before I was married with children. I was puzzled by how out of place these memories seemed, but soon I realized that I was grieving the loss of a life that was centered on meeting my own needs and having greater control over daily events.

EXERCISE: GRIEVING

Grieving allows you to enter more fully into a new phase of life. In the exercise below you will be guided toward fully grieving the transition to living a more heart-centered life. Your grieving may have stalled if you are hanging on to a life led with your rational mind. This exercise will help you ferret out what you might be hanging on to.

1. Ask yourself, "What scares me about living a heart-centered life?" In your journal, answer this question, writing as much as you can. Deborah, for example, found that living a heart-centered life would mean reorganizing her priorities in dramatic ways. She was afraid of change and found it easier to make decisions and direct her life through rational choices. In another example, it's possible that you are afraid to enter fully into your grief because you know you will encounter many previous losses that you have not yet mourned—you may fear having to face a history of buried pain.

If you do have a history of losses that are likely to come up as you evolve toward leading with your heart, you might want to consider seeking professional guidance through the process. (In addition to the books mentioned previously, some excellent resources that can support you through the process of uncovering and healing buried pain are the Health Journeys and Brain Sync audiotapes. The titles aimed at healing grief and post-traumatic stress disorder [PTSD] are especially appropriate. Even if you do not have PTSD, these tapes can be helpful in that trauma can be understood as any unresolved loss. The "Unfold Your Potential" set at www.brainsync.com can help you re-orient your life.)

2.   Next, ask yourself, "What other barriers are there to living from my heart?" In answering this question, Deborah, a doctor, found that she did not know how to tune in to her heart and let it have more of a voice in her life. As you write, allow yourself to imagine possible solutions to the problems you identify, and begin to brainstorm about how you can overcome the barriers you have identified. (If you find that, like Deborah, you do not know how to connect with your heart, you might find *The HeartMath Solution* by Childre and Martin [1999] to be helpful; this resource offers specific techniques for centering your attention and energies on your heart intelligence.)

3.   Practice tuning into your heart energies. Take a few deep breaths and connect with whatever you are feeling. Keep your attention on your heart center while imagining that you are placing your feelings aside for the time being. Assure yourself that you can return to the feeling when you have completed this experiment. Continue to allow feelings to surface and then put them aside, reassuring yourself each time that you can return to them later. With your heart center cleared, and your attention focused there, ask yourself, "What changes would I make in my life, if I lived from my heart?" Write your answers in your journal. Deborah wrote that, if she were to live from her heart, she would spend more time with each of her patients and listen to their fears about their medical conditions rather than just giving them diagnoses with prescriptions and referrals, even though this would require her to restructure her entire practice and might reduce her income.

4. Remember that the point is not to abandon living from your rational mind, but rather to integrate your head and your heart. Write a dialogue between your head and your heart in your journal. Let your head voice its fears of losing full control and give your heart a chance to respond.

5. Recognize that if you give yourself permission to lead a more heart-centered life, you will have good cause to grieve the loss of your former life, which was dominated by your rational mind. Give yourself a chance to fully grieve that loss. You may want to create a ritual or a piece of artwork to honor the transition. Deborah printed out a photo of herself and used colored markers to draw a heart on top of her head, symbolizing the integration of her heart and head. She framed the photo she had colored and hung it in a prominent place in her home to remind her of the transition she was making.

KEEP GOING

As you make the courageous journey into and through your grief, you may feel the desire to turn back. To keep going through the grief, remind yourself that in grieving one loss you are learning how to relate to all losses. The work you are doing on this loss will build your capacity to grieve losses throughout the rest of your life.

You can also remind yourself that with each layer of pain that you uncover, you are freeing yourself from the compulsion to avoid pain. (As we've discussed in earlier chapters, pain avoidance can take the form of compulsive busyness, drug or alcohol abuse, workaholism, or any other form of addiction.) You are also freeing yourself from a compulsion to re-create the pain.

The legitimate grieving you have to do in your life is persistent in its efforts to be heard. It will resurface in many forms until you honor it.

Chapter 7

Depression as Enlightenment: Embracing Emptiness

The tragedy of depression is the loss of interest in things that once enlivened. In depression, you don't care about the things that used to make you tick. Work may seem meaningless, your new car may lose its glamour, and even the thought of an upcoming vacation no longer fills you with excitement. This emptiness and meaninglessness may be quite frightening to you.

One way of looking at emptiness is to see it as something that creates a space for you to receive something new in your life. You can also see that emptiness offers you a sense of relief. When you don't care about moving ahead at work, getting that new car, or planning an exotic vacation, you finally feel unburdened by the pressures of fulfilling all of these desires. Before your depression began, you may have spent a lot of time and energy striving for new experiences, new achievements, new possessions. Your depression may be a signal that your striving has become unbalanced. Depression, and the loss of interest that comes with it, may provide a much-needed reprieve from the demands of being more and having more.

Striving for more may become an unthinking response to consumerism or competitiveness. When you lose interest in your pursuits you may begin to question why you have sacrificed so many other aspects of your life. You may find that you have abandoned your own internal compass in order to compete on a playing field defined by others.

Jane found herself sinking into depression while she was waiting tables. Although she had always enjoyed the social aspects of her job, she began to lose interest at work and had to force herself to smile. She felt like she just didn't care about making her customers happy. But when she thought seriously about quitting her job, she felt an overwhelming sense of emptiness, which frightened her. So she kept forcing herself to go to work and fake it so she wouldn't lose her job.

After some time, she began to question why she was so afraid of finding other work. She realized that her family ethic had taught her to work hard and not complain, and she had been following this ethic, even though she was tired of doing the same work. Part of her wanted to go to school to become a social worker, but she knew that in her family going to school would be considered an act of presumptuous snobbery, even a betrayal of their tough work ethic. As she contemplated leaving the playing field defined by her family, she realized she had no guidelines for how to operate in an arena where people invested in education and long-term job satisfaction.

The emptiness Jane felt was an expression of her feeling about forging her own path toward a goal that was not part of her worldview defined by her social circle. In therapy, Jane realized that the journey from the safety of the known and accepted to the risks of the unknown would require her to cross through an inner landscape of emptiness. She made a conscious choice to learn how to tolerate the emptiness so she could make the journey.

This is one of the gifts of depression. The empty feelings of depression, while uncomfortable, are part of the terrain you must cross if you are to live a life guided by a commitment to honor your own interests and energies.

A PHOBIA OF EMPTINESS

One gift of emptiness is that it allows you to avoid hardships that are caused by being phobic of emptiness. A perfect example of the hardships of being unable to tolerate emptiness is seen in the behavior of my two-year-old son as he leaves the swimming pool in the summer. He is quite happy to splash in the pool for a long time, and when he's ready he will ask to go home. After we pack up and begin to make the journey home he will invariably say, "Pool, play pool." On the first few occasions when I turned around and went back to the pool, he then said, "Home, go home, play choo choo." This could go on as long as I allowed it. As soon as I turned toward home, he wanted to play in the pool. As soon as I turned toward the pool, he wanted to go home and play with his trains. He could not tolerate the feeling of uncertainty between the pool, which he was tired of, and the trains, which he now looked forward to.

My son's dilemma is similar to that of many depressed people. The main point of this book is that depression is a signal that it's time to do something different with your life. If you hang on to a life you have outgrown and you don't take action to create a new life, depression sets in to show you the emptiness of this outmoded way of life. The problem is that when we can't tolerate the lack of certainty and comfort between the life we have outgrown and the life we are meant to live, we may spend our energies trying to get back to the old life. In order to make the transition to the new life you have to be able to tolerate the feeling of emptiness that comes from leaving that which is familiar to you.

Judy married a man she fell in love with when she was in her twenties. He was everything she ever dreamed of: he was attractive, ambitious, and the life of the party. There was never a dull moment with James. Five years later she realized that the qualities that had attracted her to James were becoming a problem: James's charming personality attracted other women, who fell prey to his charms, and James wasn't able to resist the temptation to become intimate with them. Judy knew she deserved better than to have a husband who could not be faithful to her. She experienced a depression that felt like a paralysis. She couldn't bear the idea of starting over but she knew she couldn't stay with James. Every time she took steps to separate from James she was overwhelmed with her feelings of emptiness and despair.

Her fear of emptiness kept her in a marriage she knew she had outgrown.

James's predicament was also caused by his fear of emptiness. He knew that his sexual liaisons with other women were going to lose him the person he cared most about. But after he got married he found he couldn't tolerate the emptiness he felt about leaving his old lifestyle, where his self-worth had been defined by how many women sought after him. It was easier to lose himself in the rush of excitement of his affairs. His fear of emptiness kept him cheating on his wife.

Both Judy and James were trapped by their inability to tolerate emptiness. If Judy could stay with the pain of leaving her marriage she would find the courage to create a new life. If James could tolerate the emptiness of leaving the life of a single guy he would stay faithful to his wife. Their predicament points to one way for you to think about tolerating your own emptiness: the foghorn.

EXERCISE: THE FOGHORN

A helpful metaphor for understanding emptiness is that of the foghorn. A foghorn is a haunting, wailing sound that warns people to stay away from the land during times of poor visibility and urges them to continue their journey forward. This is the role of the feeling of emptiness for you in the middle of depression. The sound of a foghorn echoes the desperation in the experience of emptiness. Rather than retreating back to the familiar when you feel that emptiness, you can learn to think of it as a warning to move away from what is familiar to you.

1. Take a moment to consciously allow yourself to feel the emptiness of your depression. Take a few deep breaths to deepen your feeling of emptiness. Go into the center of the emptiness. Try to intensify the feeling of emptiness.

2. Sit with the emptiness for as long as you can tolerate it.

3. When you feel like avoiding the emptiness, tell yourself that the emptiness is a foghorn and it is telling you to stay away from the safety of the familiar. Remind yourself that if you are to change your life you will have to cross the no-man's-land between your old life and your new life.

4. In your journal, write about what the foghorn is telling you to move away from. Is it a relationship? A professional commitment? Expectations you have always held for yourself? Allow yourself to free-associate on the image of a foghorn and what it is warning you away from.

5. As you go through your day-to-day life, every time the feeling of emptiness bothers you, remind yourself to call it a foghorn. Tell yourself, "This is a signal to move away from my old way of being."

A Gift of Depression: Originality

Emptiness will make you more original and interesting. Why? Because when you are not empty you are full—full of other people's ideas and expectations or full of your own comfortable and possibly outworn understandings. Sandra experienced this sense of emptiness after her third child started school. Previously full with the responsibilities and tasks that go along with caring for small children, she now had big spaces of empty time to fill. Having spent her entire twenties being pregnant, having babies, and taking care of young children, she took great joy in being a mother, and it was all that she knew. So when her son got on the school bus on that first day, she was filled with a sense of emptiness.

But whenever she thought about having another baby, the emptiness went away. She began thinking seriously about having another child, but her desire was met with resistance from her husband. Sandra felt depressed. Even though having another child seemed to be the answer to the pain of her emptiness, she didn't have the energy to fight her husband. She began seeing a therapist, who helped her to try interpreting the emptiness as an opening to something new. It might be an opening to a new child, or it might be an opening to something she had never considered before. She was willing to consider that her lack of energy for fighting her husband might mean that having another child was really not the answer. She began to think that if she really wanted another child she would certainly have the energy to persuade her husband.

As she practiced longer and longer periods of feeling bleak emptiness, one thought that kept returning to her was how other mothers
often asked her for fitness advice. Sandra had managed to stay very
active and fit while raising her kids, and her friends and even strangers
would ask her how she did it. Sandra decided to take her fitness to the
next level. She began training for a triathlon.

As she easily achieved her fitness goals and completed a triathlon,
Sandra came up with the idea to start a triathlon training program for
moms. This was the beginning of a new business for her, a service for
her friends and community, and it turned out to be something she
loved to do. Her accomplishments and her business challenged other
mothers to work toward greater health and fitness. Sandra had no
experience or guidance to help her start her own business, but her
willingness to tolerate the emptiness and see where it took her allowed
her to find her passion. Her emptiness challenged her to move out of
what was familiar into something different from her previous life
experiences. Her emptiness also led her out of her depression.

EXERCISE: EMPTINESS AS OPENNESS

This exercise is a companion to the first one in this chapter, in which
you learned to use the metaphor of the foghorn as a way of looking at
emptiness. In this exercise you will experiment with renaming emptiness as openness. Think of an upturned hand with nothing in it. An
open hand can be extended to receive any number of good things. The
common expression "empty handed" usually has a negative connota-
tion. This exercise will give you a tool for renaming and rethinking the
negative associations many people in our culture assign to emptiness.
You can think of it as translating your symptoms of depression into
another language that will help you make meaning of these symptoms.

1. Every time you feel the emptiness, tell yourself it is an opening to
    something new coming into your life. Think of yourself as speaking
    a new language, and translate the experience into a new language
    of "openness."

2. Practice tolerating the emptiness for longer and longer periods of
    time. When you can tolerate the emptiness for five minutes at a

time, set aside five minutes a day for one week to practice connecting with your feeling of emptiness and tolerating it.

3. After doing this successfully for one week, set aside ten minutes a day to practice sitting with your emptiness. Continue to remind yourself that the emptiness is actually openness.

4. Notice the thoughts that frequently intrude on your practice of openness. After you practice this for two weeks you may notice a theme that keeps recurring. Sandra kept returning to thoughts about her fitness and other mothers' requests for her guidance in staying fit through motherhood. This turned into an openness toward a new professional and personal vocation.

5. In your journal, write the following question at the top of a page: "What new thing am I opening up to in my life?" Write for as long as you can without inhibiting yourself.

6. In your journal, write the following question at the top of another page: "What do I have to let go of in order to allow this new thing to enter into my life?" Write for as long as you can without inhibiting yourself.

By the time you have gone through each of these steps, you may have become more comfortable with this new language for understanding your inner world. You may find that the benefits of translating emptiness into openness include not having to spend your life energy running away from the feeling of emptiness. Try to notice the behaviors you no longer seem to need. For example, you may find that you no longer need to shop as much, or you may not need your nightly glass of wine. By paying attention to naturally occurring changes in your behavior, you will increase your motivation to practice translating your symptoms of depression into meaningful experiences.

EMPTINESS: THE POWER TO RECEIVE

As you learn to be fully present with your inner sense of emptiness you will learn to translate this feeling into a reminder of your power to receive. You may receive guidance, inspiration, or a vision of a new direction in your life. Emptiness signals a willingness to receive.

You may have a hard time with this idea of passively waiting for something new to appear. Sometimes depression results from pushing too hard in many different arenas. You may be accustomed to making things happen. It is true that you need to be active, assertive, and persistent to make things happen for you. However, if you are experiencing depression, you can translate it as a way to stop pushing in the wrong direction and find a new direction.

Here's another metaphor for you to consider: think of your life journey as a mountain climbing expedition. You need to exert a lot of energy and forceful concentration in order to get where you want to go. But first you need to make sure you're taking the right trail. If you are standing in the valley, where there are many different trails you could take, you will need to pause and find some method of making a decision. Depression can be signal that you need to reconsider whether you are climbing the right mountain and following the right trail. It can mean that you need to turn inward and receive guidance about which path is in alignment with your own needs and desires.

Another metaphor for understanding the experience of emptiness is to imagine that you took a trip to an amusement park, but you didn't see any of the park's main attractions. Instead, you spent your time there going from one vending machine to another, buying sodas and snacks, not realizing that there were so many other things to see. If you did this, you would be missing the whole point of the trip—the opportunity to see spectacular shows and ride roller coasters. If you began to feel a sense of emptiness about your choice of activity, then this would a very positive signal telling you that there is something much better for you to do. Your emptiness might make you stop looking for the next vending machine and pause to reconsider what you really want to do. As you looked within you might realize that you really want to ride a roller coaster. The emptiness you felt was not a terrible symptom to push away but a gentle and sensible reminder to turn within and receive guidance about how you really want to spend your time.

In addition to receiving guidance, emptiness can be a signal telling you to transition from pushing to make things happen to waiting for something new to arrive. If you are always imposing your plans on the world, you may miss an unexpected opportunity right under your nose. This was the case for Frieda, who worked for a large corporation and was looking for a life partner. In the hopes that she would meet someone to spend her life with, she forced herself to accept as many invitations to social and business functions as she could. She dated plenty of businessmen in her field, telling herself that this was the price she had to pay in order to find a partner, but she began to feel that the endless rounds of dates with her colleagues were wearing thin. She believed she had to make things happen, but she was feeling increasingly hopeless and depressed about her failure to find happiness with the men she was meeting.

Frieda's push to find someone through her work environment made her overlook the many available men who were already in her life. She had male friends and acquaintances she enjoyed, but she rarely went out of her way to spend time with them. She didn't think she could relate to men who were not as ambitious and accomplished as she was, and she thought she would be bored with these family and high school friends, whom she had known for a long time. However, when finally she began to honor her sense of emptiness about connecting romantically with high-powered executives, she stopped forcing herself to socialize in these circles.

For many months, she felt the emptiness and hopelessness of giving up those social engagements and having nothing new in her life. But the extra time allowed her to begin hanging out with her old family friends and high-school crowd again. Through some of her best friends she met a local fireman and began dating him. She enjoyed all of her time with him, but at first she didn't really take the relationship seriously since she had never imagined herself marrying someone who wasn't in the business world.

Over time, however, she fell in love with him and understood that she wanted to spend the rest of her life with him. Because he was so different from her, Freida found herself fascinated by him. She realized why she was so bored with dating businessmen (they were too similar to her and didn't offer her anything new). She also respected how brave and courageous her new partner was, and she admired that he served his community selflessly.

As she reflected on her own surprise about her happiness with her partner, she recognized that she had had to go through the emptiness of giving up her expectations about the ideal life partner in order to find someone who brought something radically new into her life. She also began to bring her own life in line with the things she really valued—enjoying nature and physical activity. She saw that she had neglected so many areas of her life in the service of her exclusive focus on her work life and romantic ambitions.

NO SUCH THING AS EMPTINESS

As you are making your way through the difficulties of feelings of emptiness, despair, or disorientation, you may find it helpful to remind yourself that from a philosophical standpoint, emptiness does not exist. For example, an empty bowl is not really empty: it's filled with oxygen particles and air, which is essential to life.

Many times you may feel empty after a loss, a failure, or a rejection. When something has left your life it is natural to feel like there is nothing else there. But in reality your life is always enormously full. If you lose a job, you still have your relationships. If you lose a relationship, you still have other relationships. If you lose money, you still have your gifts and talents. If you lose your health, you still have relationships or professional vocations. If you lose almost everything, you can still go to the library and read books to inspire or comfort you. In short, there is always something there—it's just a matter of how you perceive it.

SECURITY GUARDING

Ultimately, the sense of emptiness is about a loss of control and security. Your life feels empty when your plans for how your life will unfold are challenged, and you feel less than confident. Emptiness can also be about the lack of confidence in your own gifts and abilities. If you are rejected by someone, you naturally feel a sense of emptiness. However, if you felt full of all your attractive qualities, you would realize that one rejection doesn't take anything away from who you are; it only takes one person out of your life. If you were not chosen for a job you wanted, it wouldn't take away any of your skills, talents, or gifts. It would just take away one specific job possibility.

The deeper meaning of emptiness can be to help you connect with your deepest gifts and talents—both personal and professional— which transcend any specific person, place, or opportunity.

Opportunities will come and go, but your many attractive qualities will always be there, and as a result you will always be full no matter what losses or failures you experience. The following exercise can help you to find meaning—and fullness—in your emptiness when faced with loss or failure.

EXERCISE: FINDING MEANING IN LOSS

1. Try on the following ways of making meaning of rejection, failure, or loss. Take out your journal and write the following statements, each at the top of a page:

   The meaning of this emptiness is to show me that my life is already full.

   The meaning of emptiness is to help me appreciate everything else in my life.

   The meaning of my emptiness is to show me my gifts that transcend any situation.

   Even if you don't believe these statements are true, suspend your disbelief for this exercise and write in your journal all the ways that these statements could be true.

2. Write the following statement at the top of another page in your journal:

   I am bigger than _____ . (Fill in the blank with whatever event has caused the loss, such as the end of a relationship, or a troublesome health problem.)

   The reason this has left my life is so something better can come into my life.

   It doesn't matter if you believe these statements to be true. In your journal, write all the evidence you have that shows these statements are true. Also write about your expectations for the future, assuming that these statements are true.

3. Each time you feel anxiety about the emptiness in your life, acknowledge that it is a natural, predictable reaction to any loss or

change. And if it is true that emptiness is also an openness to something new coming into your life, then you have something to look forward to. Tell yourself that if your life is to continue to get bigger, you have to seek out anxiety rather than avoid it. Once you have accepted and honored your anxiety, practice translating it into excitement by simply saying to yourself:

"This openness will permit something new to come into my life. I can't wait to find out what is coming."

Remember the axiom "Nature abhors a vacuum"? If you create a space for honoring the emptiness, something new must enter into your life. Think of Frieda, who, in honoring her sense of emptiness about dating her professional colleagues, found love with someone outside of her familiar realm and began to develop parts of herself that had been lying dormant.

The Emptiness of Control and Security

As we discussed above, when you explore your feelings of emptiness, what you may find is that the foundation of these feelings is the loss of a sense of control and security. However, it is the belief in control and security that is empty. You are never in complete control, nor do you have any guaranteed security. Your feelings of emptiness reflect the reality that change is a part of life and that lasting security is a comforting delusion.

Many people who are depressed compare their current feelings with the feelings they remember from their previous life and make themselves more depressed. For example, you may believe that before you were depressed you had it all together, had a sense of security and safety, and felt like you were in control of your life. You can stop yourself from increasing your unnecessary suffering about your depression by recognizing that you were never in control in the first place.

Psychologists believe that depressed people actually perceive the world more accurately than those who are not depressed, a perception called "depressive realism" (Alloy and Abrahamson 1998). This may sound even more depressing, but think of it this way: your feeling of being out of control in your depression is really a more accurate perception of your reality as it has always been. You can stop blaming yourself for the loss of control you are experiencing in your depression. You didn't lose control—you never had it, or at least you didn't have as much control as you thought.

Your depression may have been triggered by a life event (such as a failure, a significant loss, or a rejection) that led to a loss of security. You may be increasing your suffering if you compound your depression by focusing on the security you believe you have lost. The more you can recognize that life by its very nature is not secure, the more you can let go of some of your angst, and transform your depression into a gift. If in fact you did have more control and security, your life would probably be stale. As Hugh Prather wrote in *Notes to Myself*, "Perfectionism is a slow death. . . . If everything were to turn out just as I would want it, just as I would plan, I would never experience anything new. My life would be an endless repetition of stale successes. When I make a mistake I experience something unexpected" (1983, p. 21). So it may be just an illusion that more control makes for a better life. If you can change your beliefs so that you actually desire insecurity and seek experiences outside of your comfort zone, you will find the meaning in your depression. This is because the message of depression usually pushes you toward a new life.

EXERCISE: BECOME AN EXPERIENCE COLLECTOR

1. If you're struggling with this idea that before your depression you did not have all that much control and security in your life, then you should examine what is really true about your previous life. Ask yourself the following questions and write your reflections in your journal:

   ■ Was I calm and serene before my depression?

   ■ What did I worry about before my depression?

   ■ What did I feel out of control about before my depression?

■   What did I feel insecure about before my depression?

2.   Many times the suffering associated with feeling out of control is caused by a mental comparison between the current feeling of little control and an ideal state of having perfect control. But there is no such state of perfect control. Read and contemplate the following paragraph, and consider it a challenge to the idea that your highest value is to seek control and security:

Imagine that a great healer comes to you and tells you that your purpose in life is to always seek out new experiences. Your life is intended to be an exploration of what it means to be fully human. This healer connects you with the part of yourself that sees your life as an exciting playing field where you can discover new aspects of the world, yourself, and other people. This part of yourself values venturing out of your comfort zone more than it values security and control.

Experiment with trying on a new core value and see how it affects your depression and attitude toward change. Sometimes in your depression you may agonize over the senseless suffering your depression seems to have caused. The above exercise will help relieve some of that agony by helping you see the bigger picture.

VAST WORLD, SHORT LIFE

There is a part of you that recognizes the vastness of the world and the shortness of your life and wants you to taste as many experiences as possible. You want to meet new people, try out different jobs, explore different lifestyles, and experience the full range of possibilities. This part of yourself welcomes every change, because of the new experiences that are certain to follow.

Like a teenager backpacking through Europe trying to seek out the new and the different, you anticipate each new transition for all that it will bring into your life. As much as you have enjoyed Paris and long to stay there, if you never left you would miss out on the south of France, Spain, Portugal, Italy, Germany, Greece, and all they have to offer. As you imagine with great certainty that exploring your world is the meaning of your life, ask yourself how this transforms your experience of the changes in your life.

With this most radical perspective, you may even view your depression as a common human passage that is worthwhile for you to go through. If you are a person who is seeking out human experiences, then depression is one stop on a tour of all that makes us human. To avoid depression would mean depriving yourself of the experiences of grief, emptiness, and pain. Your depression is not the end of the road; it is, rather, part of the journey.

Chapter 8

Depression as an Expansion of the Allowable

When you're depressed life may seem bleak. You may feel indifferent to many things that once held a great deal of interest for you. You may lose interest in old friends. Some of your cherished goals may no longer seem worthwhile. You may lose your enthusiasm for your work and find yourself just dragging through your day.

In this chapter you will learn how to analyze the pattern of your lost interests in order to create a different life. Once you have traversed through your emptiness, you have created a space for something new to enter. Now your symptoms of indifference—not caring what others think, not caring about your goals, not caring about your social connections—will help you choose what will fill your newly created empty space.

How does this work? Imagine that you have finally thrown out your junky old hand-me-down furniture. You now have a room that is empty and ready to be refurnished and redecorated. What will you fill the room with?

In order to fill the room with furniture that you love and that represents your own unique tastes and preferences, you will have to permit yourself the fullest expression of your deepest inclinations—you will find your true personal atmosphere. Depression, which makes you indifferent to the old rules that used to guide your life, is what makes this possible.

You will likely have to expand your sense of what is allowable to find and express your own tastes. You may find this challenging, especially if you have borrowed someone else's sense of style because your own tastes clash with rigid beliefs or cultural expectations. For example, when Francine framed her depression as an opportunity to "refurnish" her life, she pictured herself decorating it with paintings of female nudes. She had used her depression to come to terms with her interest in other women. Her feelings of indifference to many aspects of her previous life gave her the breathing space to begin to allow her new life to emerge.

YOUR PERSONAL ATMOSPHERE

Your personal atmosphere is what is most unique about you. It is the energy you exude and the way people feel when they come into your orbit. Think of the atmosphere that you experience in different restaurants. You have a choice: do you want to be like a fast-food restaurant that is pretty much the same no matter where you go all over the globe, or do you want to be like a new and interesting restaurant with a completely original menu?

Everyone's personal atmosphere is different. Your atmosphere has a dominant theme and emotional tone. During your depression, your personal atmosphere is under construction. You are in the process of reevaluating your life to allow a deeper expression of your peculiarities and eccentricities. That which you used to sweep under the rug you may now bring out into the open. This process will create a more inviting atmosphere. The more you are struggling to live according to rigid expectations, which means you must necessarily hide the more interesting parts of yourself, the more tension you will feel and the more tension will be felt by others in your atmosphere.

The tension of repressing yourself has negative consequences for your life. The constant effort of trying to be something you are not, and trying not to be something you are, takes its toll. Your relationships, health, and work life may suffer.

EXERCISE: MAKING A CENTERPIECE OF WHAT IS HIDDEN

This exercise will help you connect with your personal atmosphere. Many times the most powerful and compelling expression of your personal atmosphere comes from bringing out into the open something you have been ashamed of. Francine, who wanted to decorate her home with female nudes, had an atmosphere that was distinctly unique, but she had been hiding this important part of herself. On a purely pragmatic level, her lack of self-acceptance made it difficult for her to have a relationship with another woman. If she had been open about her interest in other women, she might have found a relationship more easily and stopped wasting her time trying to maintain her romantic relationships with men.

1. Imagine you had an empty room in your home to decorate. What would give that room the most energy? What would you secretly desire to be the main theme of the room? What would you be most afraid to have in the room?

2. Use your answers to the question above to select a theme that is important to you but that you are not fully expressing in your life right now. Joelle, for example, wrote that she would like to decorate her room with African art. In reviewing her responses, she realized that she had not been fully expressing her deep interest in her African heritage, even though it was intensely compelling to her.

3. Ask yourself how you can make this personal quality or theme a bigger part of your life. Take action to bring more of this quality or theme into your life. Joelle stopped taking Yoga classes, which were popular among her friends, and instead found an African drumming class. She also signed up for a class on African

American history at her local college, and she started organizing Black History Month events in her community to honor her heritage and share it with others. As Joelle began to make her African heritage a centerpiece in her life, she felt more alive than she had in a long time. This reorientation of her personal and social life around her interest in African art, music, and culture led to a dramatic lessening of her depression. Her more-developed personal atmosphere affected her family, too. Her children loved having their mother seem so vitalized. Her husband also enjoyed having a new focus for family activities.

THE MEANING OF SHAME

A common symptom of depression is constant self-recrimination. You may criticize yourself frequently. You may feel ashamed of yourself, like you can never do anything right. Sometimes you may feel like you want to sink into the earth and hide your face. Shame can be an indicator of your deepest yearnings. Because so many people have had their dreams and hidden aspirations be ridiculed by others, they may internalize a sense of shame about what they really want to do. In *The Secret Message of Shame*, the authors write that "paradoxically, then, shame serves as a marker for hidden yearnings. That which you are ashamed of may be exactly that for which you yearn. . . . That means that sometimes instead of hiding in avoidance, you must journey through the desert of shame in order to reach the promised land of your yearnings" (Potter-Efron and Potter-Efron 1999, p. 67).

You can learn to transform your shame into a meaningful message to you. Shame shows you where you are called to challenge your current definitions of normality. You can learn to translate shame into an indicator telling you to push past your current limitations imposed by your need for conformity.

In creating your own original personal atmosphere, it is predictable that at times you will dare to challenge your expectations rather than conform to them. Shame means you have arrived at the boundary separating where you feel comfortable and where you are meant to go.

Shame calls you to expand your sense of the allowable—and maybe even to take others with you.

However, there is one important exception to this advice: if you have been a victim of sexual, emotional, or physical abuse, then you may need treatment for trauma. In that case, your symptoms of depression may actually be related to post-traumatic stress disorder (PTSD), and therefore the themes in this book may not apply quite as well to your experience. If you have suffered a traumatic event and may have PTSD, it is important not to confuse this disorder with a major depression. The more severe the trauma, the more urgent is your need for professional support to help you work through your major symptoms.

In cases other than victimization, shame is a signal for you to push past where you are and start moving toward where you are meant to go. If you avoid confronting your shame you may end up failing to create the one-of-a-kind personal atmosphere that you are meant to have. Shame is an invitation, calling you away from the safe and secure.

Marcus felt intense shame when he became emotional in his corporate work setting. It threatened his sense of masculinity and his need to be in total control. Each time he opened up to his coworkers about his family stressors, he felt that he had revealed too much.

In therapy, Marcus learned to perceive the feeling of shame as a signal to forge his own path even in the face of the hard-nosed ethos at work, which made emotional expression seem indecent. Guided by the signals telling him to push through his shame, he began to experiment with expressing his emotions about conditions at work. Taking small steps and tracking the outcomes, he found that he was beginning to form important alliances among his coworkers. Others began to turn to him, too, and he felt more alive as he became a person who was building a sense of community where previously most people had felt alienated. Soon he found that not only was he enjoying work much more but he was also using it to discover his own gifts and explore new ways of being in the world.

You may think that the problems you are forced to confront on a daily basis are an obstacle to achieving your life purpose. In fact, the problems that cross your path are directing you toward exactly where you can be of most service. The skills and talents that you develop while coping with the most troublesome of problems are a good indication of the direction you can move in so that you can most effectively utilize your natural gifts.

The skills and talents Marcus developed involved expanding his capacity for emotional expression in order to cope with family- and work-related problems. This expanded capacity provided a much-needed resource for everyone who came within his orbit. He served as both a role model and a leader in his ability to connect with many different people. His shame was a reflection of his accurate perception that it was not "normal" in his corporate culture to express his emotions.

A contribution is by definition bringing something new and valuable to one's community. Whenever you add something new, you push the limits of what is accepted. For this reason, your shame can be a signal that you are on the verge of making your greatest contribution and finding your unique value. The very actions for which you recriminate yourself the most may be those that would allow you to make your greatest contribution.

However, there is a difference between shame and guilt. It is important that you are able to distinguish between the two before going on to the next exercise. If you feel guilt, then you can identify the behavior that is causing the guilt and stop the behavior; once you have done this, you can expect the guilt to go away. Of course, if the behavior involves an abuse of power, exploitation, or emotional, physical, or sexual mistreatment of someone else, then these destructive behaviors should clearly be stopped. These behaviors should naturally generate guilt in the perpetrator. However, if you can be sure that no other person is being victimized by the action but rather that the behavior is only causing an internal or external rule to be broken, then the following exercise can help you translate some of the self-recrimination you feel into a useful emotion so that you can reach your greatest potential.

EXERCISE: BEING PROUD OF FEELING MORTIFIED

I. Think of the last time you felt ashamed, or berated yourself for acting in ways that were not "normal." In your journal, write what you did. Write about what you felt for doing this. Write all the things you said to yourself about your behavior.

Maya remembered feeling ashamed of herself for not helping a friend move out of her apartment. When Maya had told her that she could not help, her friend had gotten mad. Maya wrote down all the thoughts she had said to herself, including the following:

"I'm selfish. I can't even help a friend."

"No one will ever help me now since I'm so mean."

"I don't deserve to have any friends."

"I'll never have any friends if I can't be generous."

2. How can you translate your feeling of shame into a signal that you need to create a new rule for yourself and others? Write in your journal any ideas that come to mind. Maya wrote in her journal that it was okay for her to say no to her friend, and that she could make a contribution by showing others, through her own behavior, how to take care of themselves. She realized that by taking care of herself, she was showing other people how to treat her. By respecting her own limitations, others would respect her more. She also saw that she didn't have to take care of her friend, even if she was angry. She realized that she had to forge a new path and stop believing that she had to help everyone and take care of them.

3. Read through what you have written and create the boldest statements you can about the new rules you are creating for yourself. Maya came up with the following:

New Rule 1: I'm allowed to set limits.

New Rule 2: I don't have to take care of others.

New Rule 3: If others are upset by my new rules, they are capable of dealing with it themselves. I don't have to make it better for them.

New Rule 4: Other people are responsible for their own upsets and emotional states.

4. Experiment with your new rules and keep track of how these changes affect your depression. If you find yourself moving away from your depression and experience relief from it, that means you have heard the message in your depression and you will no longer

need the symptoms to provide guidance and force you to reflect on your life. It means you are moving in the right direction.

ANGER, ANGST, AND OTHER THINGS

Here's something to think about: the very efforts we make to hide things we are ashamed of—anger, angst, and other feelings—limit our capacity to relate to others. Research has shown that women who report the highest levels of marital satisfaction are more likely to show anger behaviors such as being critical toward their spouses and withdrawing at the end of a bad day (Schulz et al. 2004).

We feel shame when we want to hide something. If we follow the dictates of our shame, our ability to relate to others and have others relate to us will be minimal. It is for this reason that you will benefit by translating your shame into a signal to move forward and challenge the internalized rule that is causing the shame. At the very least you will want to use your shame as a signal to reflect on what rule has been broken. It might be a core value that is central to your integrity and one you want to maintain. In that case, the feeling will be one of guilt, and once you address the wrong, the guilt for violating your own standards and values should go away. However, depression is characterized by a paralyzing sense of shame and self-recrimination that is not righted when corrective action is taken. It is therefore a call to reflect on the rules that are restricting your life and consider whether they should be challenged.

There is a very practical reason to express the anger, sadness, or other emotions that you may want to hide. If you don't share your anger at your partner, friend, or coworker, you do not give that person an opportunity to solve the problem that has sparked the anger.

While all relationships must be built on positive emotions of love, attraction, respect, and tenderness, these emotions can only be maintained if there is the possibility of correcting things when they veer off course. Anger, sadness, irritation, and other emotions offer an opportunity to communicate and give your partner a chance to address your concerns.

Intimacy is impossible if you live in fear of revealing all aspects of yourself—your love, your needs, your rages, your doubts. We all hate the feeling that another is keeping something from us, because it represents a lack of sharing. The simple act of withholding anger in a relationship can set in motion vicious cycles of withholding, withdrawal, and further withholding, ultimately leading to tension and a lack of authenticity that frequently causes the relationship to fail. Shame is often the signal that you are at a place where you can grow. By making changes in your inner world, you can push past your comfort zone and transform your life.

EXPANSION OF THE ALLOWABLE

The meaning of your depression may be to make your current, limiting beliefs so painful that you are forced to reconsider ways to expand and live beyond those beliefs. The gift in your depression is that by hearing its message and finding the meaning in it, your life will expand. You may find yourself on a much larger playing field or living a life of greater ease.

There is some predictability in the limiting beliefs we hold, since many such beliefs are culturally determined. If you are too depressed to follow the exercises, below is a "cheat sheet" of common beliefs you might consider challenging:

- I need to be in control of everything, all the time.

- No one will like me if I show them how I really feel.

- I can't say no.

- It's easier to just say yes than to set limits.

- I'm afraid of change.

- Everything has to be a struggle.

- I should only feel loving and caring in intimate relationships.

New Rules

If you find yourself ashamed of many of your feelings, or if you have a difficult time knowing what you feel, you might try experimenting with some of the following replacement rules:

- I can feel as mad as I want for as long as I want.

- I can feel as afraid as I want for as long as I want.

- I can feel as sad as I want for as long as I want.

- I can feel as happy as I want for as long as I want.

- I can wake up excited every day.

- I can make mistakes.

- I can create my own rules.

This final rule is the most important rule. It gives you permission to author your own rules, to become your own authority. Creating your own rules is a scary process, and you may experience consequences that result in major life changes.

It may be that, if not for depression, few people would ever venture out to explore the world beyond their inherited beliefs. The fact is that it is much easier to live your life with the current expectations and rules. To rewrite your rules and live outside the accepted guidelines is to invite the possibility of making terrible mistakes, or even just small mistakes. When you write your own rules and then you mess up, you only have yourself to blame. When you follow someone else's rules and mess up, you have an easy out—you can blame someone else. But if you are struggling with depression, think of it as nature's way of forcing you out of your comfort zone, by making your comfort zone, well, depressing, and spurring you to live the life you're meant to live.

Chapter 9

Depression as Freedom from Seeking Approval

As you begin to write and live by your own rules, the feeling of not caring what other people think permits you to expand your sense of what is allowable and experiment with new ways of being in the world. Thus, the feeling of being indifferent to what other people think of you marks the turning point in the work of depression. In the last chapter you worked on making an internal shift by writing new rules. In this chapter you will learn how to handle the response from the external world. You can bet that failures and rejection will cross your path as you make changes in your life that affect the outer world.

Your symptoms of depression may help you push through these painful realities. Many people with depression complain that they feel worthless or not valued. These feelings of worthlessness, when combined with not caring what other people think, can free you from the need to have approval from others in your environment. The intense feelings of worthlessness provide an immunization of sorts to being crushed by failure and rejection. If your depression makes you feel worthless, then you will not change your course when other people reject you. In short, the more familiar you are with feeling worthless, the less likely you are to be moved by the actions of others who do not value you.

Think of a person who has never been through depression. This person may have never felt "like a winter-hardened piece of shit," as one of my clients described it. A person who has never felt bad about herself and has never learned to pick herself up and keep going might be extremely sensitive to negative feedback. A single rejection could be a devastating blow.

In contrast, a depressed person who has gone through the struggle to tolerate feeling worthless will be more resistant to rejection. For a person who has stopped caring what other people think and has felt bad about herself for long periods of time, the painful events of the world will have less power to knock her down. (Note that there is a subtype of depression in which people are more sensitive to rejection, and this discussion may be less relevant for that subtype.)

Looking at the way many people lead their lives, one might guess that the dirtiest word in the English language is a four-letter word that starts with F: "fail." Many people lead their lives with the singular mission of avoiding failure. Depression may be an effort to challenge the rigid limitations imposed on a life that is guided by such a narrow mission. Depression is the predictable result of compulsively analyzing yourself, pushing and pulling yourself into shape, and not daring to take a wrong step. Depression is trying to free you to see that there is no danger of making a mistake: all of your actions, choices, and life experiences are forms of self-expression.

The consequences of living a life guided by the ideal of not making a mistake is that you become a constrained, overcontrolled, tensed-up ball of fear. This can cause enormous tension that sets up an interesting dynamic that compels you to make catastrophic mistakes in order to free yourself from the ever-present danger of "making a mistake." You can then begin to think of yourself as a collector of experiences. Making mistakes is a hallmark of human experience. What is called a mistake may be a daring expression of your own being interacting with a world that needs to be changed. Roger Housden, in *Seven Sins for a Life Worth Living,* called mistakes "our own contribution to global diversity" (2005b, p. 117).

Similarly, depression may free you up to make mistakes. Your lack of interest, motivation, and concern about what other people think may permit you the space you need to begin to experiment with your life. If you can translate your depression into freedom to experiment, you can transform your life from a constant struggle to an opportunity to play and create. You can give yourself permission to feel like a young child plunging his hands into finger paint and smearing it on paper with delight. The creation of your life can be playful art. Its grandeur will be found in its breathtaking originality—not in its technical perfection, beaten into shape through years of reform school. Even when your experimentation leads to failure, with the right attitude these experiences can contribute to your own greater good.

THE POWER OF DEFEAT

Depression predictably results when your fear of admitting to a mistake is so great that you persist in maintaining an intolerable situation. Acknowledging that you made a choice that you would now like to change can free you so you can move your life forward. In your depression, you may berate yourself for your errors. But if you give yourself permission to realize that a wrong choice allowed you to gain experiences you otherwise would not have had, then you can stop beating yourself up and get on with your life.

Adam left his wife of twenty years to marry Michelle, a younger woman who made him feel alive. A year after he married Michelle, he began to realize that he could not live with her. She wasn't able to take care of herself, and she wasn't interested in exploring the world or finding a professional vocation. He had fallen in love with her because she had made him the center of her world; now, the very thing that had attracted him had become an intense burden. The pressure he felt to support her in the lifestyle she expected was forcing him to give up his own dreams.

He was particularly loath to admit that his second marriage wasn't going to work, because everyone had told him he was making a mistake. His divorce had been bitter and almost everything his ex-wife had said about Michelle had turned out to be true. Admitting failure would mean acknowledging that both his divorce and his second marriage were mistakes. He couldn't stand the idea.

As Adam's sense of despair increased, he began to stop caring what anybody thought of him. He could not care less if his ex-wife was proved right, and he didn't care if everyone in the world thought he was an idiot. He began to realize that it was more important to free himself up than to avoid the appearance of making a stupid mistake.

In therapy, he practiced viewing his choices as important life experiences rather than as meaningless mistakes. If his purpose was more about collecting human experiences rather than avoiding mistakes, he could acknowledge that he had experienced intense highs and lows in the last few years of his life. He had felt like the happiest guy in the world when he was in love with Michelle. He had felt rejuvenated and had realized that even at his age he could connect with new and interesting people. Later, he had felt like the biggest jerk in the world for leaving his first wife and for deciding not to stay with his second wife. He had experienced love and love lost, two universal themes in the human condition.

As he began to rechart his life course, he felt a permission to try new things since he had already made a fool of himself. The painful worthlessness of his depression made him realize that he could take it if everyone learned how badly he had messed up. No longer would he be haunted by the feeling that he had to watch his every step—he had already messed up big and survived to tell about it. He was able to recall the exhilaration he had felt at his newfound love and reclaim that as an attitude toward life. He didn't need Michelle to feel that life was open with possibilities—he could create that feeling on his own.

Adam's story illustrates how depression can free a person to admit a mistake and move on. If he had persisted in maintaining the illusion that his second marriage was a good choice, he only would have hurt himself. In his despair, when he stopped caring what anyone thought, he found the power to lead his life on his own terms.

Adam also found another reason to acknowledge his error. By admitting his mistake, he would be teaching his children the lesson he had learned—that it's only human to make mistakes. In incorporating this lesson into his life, he freed up his children from the pressures of trying to be perfect. This freedom helped his son relax as he was deciding what job he should take after high school. Adam got him to see that he would gain interesting experiences at many different jobs, and that he could think of each job as an opportunity to experiment rather than as an iron-clad decision about what to do with the rest of his life. Adam's ability to face his mistake didn't affect just his children—it also allowed him for the first time to apologize to his ex-wife. This was a tremendous gift to her, which helped her in her own healing process.

THE MEANING IN THE MISTAKE

The meaning behind failure and mistakes can be that you need to wake up from your competitive trance. If you are spending precious life energy trying to win competitions that are not in line with who you are and who you want to be, then failure and mistakes can be a gift that causes you to reevaluate your competitiveness. This can take the form of "keeping up with the Joneses" but it also can be much more subtle and pervasive.

Every environment you find yourself in will have some form of competitiveness at work. What people are competing for may differ wildly, but the underlying competition is present. A friend of mine, who once went from working in a prestigious law firm to working as a waitress in one week, remarked at how all of a sudden the rules had changed from vying to put in the most billable hours to vying to wear the shortest skirt. Competition was a major factor in both environments, but the golden ring was different.

If you are in an environment that was meant to be a stepping-stone, or was an experiment to find out how you would like it, it can be difficult to ever leave. You may get caught up in the competition and forget to constantly monitor the environment to make sure it is in line with your highest vision for yourself. If you get caught up in such a position, mistakes and failures may be just what you need—they may get you going on a vision quest to figure out what you really want.

Deborah Harper, president of Psychjourney, wrote me about her own experience with depression and mistakes, which led her to create a Web site (www.psychjourney.com) that would be a resource for families in distress who are seeking the best in mental health services. She writes:

> When my family finally emerged from the two-year crisis of dealing with our daughter's drug addiction, recovery, and family healing, I made a vow that I would dedicate the rest of my life to helping other families in crisis find the help they needed.
> I knew there had to be a better way of selecting a therapist, psychiatrist, marriage counselor, and drug treatment center than the desperate searching based on minimal information that we and so many other families we knew had experienced. I had an inkling that somehow the Internet would provide the answer. Beyond that, I could only move in faith.

I took the risk of quitting my job, going back to school for two years to study computers and to gain other skills I knew I needed. After completing my studies I took a job to help pay the bills. My year of work was interesting and rewarding but I found myself getting frequently depressed and making stupid mistakes on the job. I could not figure out what was going on, since I had chosen to be there and had always been very conscientious on any job I undertook. In retrospect, I realize that the mistakes were a message to devote my time fully to further gather the skills I needed to create Psychjourney.

Looking back I realize my depression, anxiety, and self-sabotage on the job were a result of my inner knowledge that my full-time work and four-hour-a-day commute made it impossible to fulfill the vow I made. It was very difficult to leave a paid job when we badly needed the money—we had two children in college—and I was leaving for a vision that no one outside my family understood or supported.

It was and is difficult to explain how I could dedicate years to a project that was risky, had not been done before, and had no clear model for financial success. The Jones family has no worries about keeping up with us.

To keep myself centered and aligned with my vision and life path, I have had to let go of my need to be considered a success in conventional terms. As I come from a very materialistic, competitive, career-driven family and live in an area with the highest cost and standard of living nationwide, this has been challenging.

But most importantly I have realized that success for me is fulfilling the vow I made and working every day to make my vision manifest. It helps me to stay centered to look back on how far my family has come.

During our daughter's three-week stay in a lockdown psychiatric hospital after a psychotic break, a staff psychologist there told me that Rachael was a high-suicide risk and that I should prepare myself for her death. She is now a full-time student in chemistry at a major university, is in a healthy five-year relationship, and has been clean and sober for the past ten years.

Our son, Michael, who at thirteen experienced his family falling apart as we struggled with his sister's addiction, is a full-time graduate student, does work he loves in his field, and also just celebrated five years with the woman he loves.

My marriage, which I feared would end because of the stress of our family crisis, is happy and strong. We just celebrated our thirtieth year of marriage.

Every day I get up and am able to work full-time on building Psychjourney. I have the privilege of meeting incredible people from all over the world who share the dream and give generously of their time and expertise. Every day hundreds of people from all over the world visit our Web site or blog and listen to our audio files. And we have just started.

And when my time on earth is done, I will be able to look back and say I did everything in my power to keep the sacred vow I made. This to me is success.

Deborah's story illustrates the central gift of depression. It effectively "forces" a person to create his own rules, to author his own life. Claiming such authority flies in the face of cultural values and family expectations. Deborah's depression in part led her to a vision of a meaningful life of helping others rather than conforming to expectations that she achieve material success in conventional terms.

Because the pain of walking your own path can be so difficult, depression gives you a push from what used to be your comfort zone, by making you lose interest in conventional goals, values, and expectations.

EXERCISE: VISION QUESTING

For the following exercise, think of a mistake that haunts you. The following series of questions will help you use this mistake to gain increased clarity about your true life path.

1. Ask yourself, "If this mistake is in alignment with my highest vision of my life and its possibilities, what is the meaning of the mistake?"

2. Ask yourself, "If the events of my life are meant to be my personal guru, what message is my guru giving me about the direction I should take at this point in my life?"

Imagine you went to the holiest guru in the world and asked her, "What is the meaning of my life?" Imagine that her answer was "Wait and see. Your life will speak to you." Then imagine that the mistake you identified before beginning this exercise occurred. What would it mean? Remember that the purpose could be to reconnect you with bigger and better goals or help you build important skills that are essential to the contribution you need to make to the world.

3. Ask yourself, "What lessons am I learning from this failure or mistake? What skills am I learning from these events?"

4. Based on your responses to these questions, write out a summary statement of your own guiding vision. What are you working toward? Who are you meant to be?

5. If you find yourself getting stuck and dwelling on your mistake, you may want to reflect on the general attitude you are taking toward yourself. One way to change your attitude is to change the questions you ask yourself. To find the meaning in the mistake you will have to stop asking yourself questions like "Who is to blame?" "What did I do to deserve this?" and "What's wrong with me?" To try to overcome any tendency to self-punish, ask yourself the following questions:

Am I okay?

What do I need?

How can I comfort myself?

IN THE DARKEST HOUR

When the pain of depression rips apart your life, the vision of what you are supposed to do with your life may show itself as the only thing that sustains you through your depression. In the midst of deepest despair, a guiding vision may appear. From listening to the stories people and clients have shared with me, I have come to see depression as an obscuring of everything except what is absolutely essential.

Depression may be like a switch that makes all the lights go out in order to reveal what is already shining. When the lights are on and you are not depressed you can see many things. When the lights go off, you can see only that which is lit from within. Usually what you will find is the meeting place where both your gifts and the thing the world needs from you come together in a perfect calling or mission—which almost always seems like a "mission impossible." Let's look at Jaime's story, which illustrates how the light can be found in the darkest hour. Jaime Buckley created the first online comic book, WANTED: HERO (www.wantedhero.com), and earns a living supporting his family by doing what he loves.

How did I get here?

I look back at my own life, and when I calmly observe all the factors . . . I would have to say, I arrived at this very day by nothing short of a miracle. I personally believe that miracle was called "depression." I know it sounds strange, and [you might] think me insane, but I assure you, depression is exactly what I suffered from, and it is a key factor in changing my life for the better.

I was raised in a very loving home and married a wonderful, loving wife. However, I had many expectations out of life, expectations that I traded, to be a "loyal" person, and placed that "service of loyalty" (to friends, family, and associates) above my own feelings, my own needs, and even those of the needs of my dependents. Almost without exception, to my great dismay and pain, the people around me, and those I gave my loyalty to, did not see it as a valued gift . . . and I would be taken advantage of, in many ways.

The other, painful aspect of this life I seemed to carve for myself was that I became naturally dependent upon those I was loyal to. I graduated high school at fifteen, with honors and credits towards college. I had several scholarships available to me . . . yet I chose to stay near my father and work side by side, figuring I could go later. I never went. As time went by, I depended more and more on my ability

to be loyal and "watch someone's back" (dispel rumors, be
there to assist the person when in need, work incredibly long
hours at meaningless jobs that no one else would do, even
place myself in harm's way to protect them or their family).
I began to value myself less and less, and after a time
classified myself as "substandard" to everyone else.

In my mind, I was an uneducated, unskilled, hopeless
case—who felt, even worse, that my wife had been so wrong
about me, and married far beneath her own worth. I knew,
that should I ever become obsolete to the one I was loyal to,
I wouldn't have a place to turn, no direction . . . and all
would be lost. I wouldn't be able to support myself, or get
a job to take care of my growing family.

This whole time, year after year after year . . . I felt
this pressure build up inside me, that caused severe pain and
health problems, many of which took such a toll on me that
they still ail me today. It got to a point that I lost all hope,
all feeling, all desire to survive . . . the pressure ever
increasing . . . until it became so intense, I thought I was
going to die from the sheer pain in my head and heart.

I remember a burst of anger. Not a temper, but an
anger like I had never known . . . something I might liken to
"righteous indignation" . . . about my life, where I was, and
the lack of my direction. Thoughts and feelings flooded my
body with such clarity . . . and the weight started to ease.
All that remained was the fear. A fear that told me a huge
change was about to take place . . . a change that was
necessary for my survival and the future of my own family.

Over the next days, weeks, and months, I noticed
more, felt more, and realized that I always had the ability
to progress on my own—[I always had] talents to make a
living—but I never allowed myself the right to do it. It was
like if I did something for myself, I would be betraying the
"loyalty" side of my nature. The funny thing was, not long
after, I realized that I had based my loyalty upon myself,
and not the actions of others. I had failed to qualify people
for that loyalty, and it had nearly destroyed me.

I saw that I had a wonderful wife and amazing
children, who not only loved me . . . they had always loved
me. For me. Just plain old me. Imagine that! I had never

noticed until then. Once I gave myself permission to live my life, and to strive to become more than I had limited myself to be, my health improved, ideas began to flow, and I developed a hunger to take it even farther.

I wanted to take my deepest love . . . telling stories to children and drawing cartoons, to a new level of development. I wanted to make a living with it. I didn't believe anyone like Marvel or DC would hire me . . . but I had learned enough while being a shadow to other successful people over the years to strike out on my own! I could be original. I knew how to do that! I talked it over with my wife and children, who gave me their encouragement and support, grabbed my tax refund of $1,000, and started my own comic book company. However, I still lacked $135 needed for supplies, with no way to attain it.

My mother had been killed the year before, and I had yet to break down and mourn her loss . . . which was creating anger again in my life. A friend suggested I go out to Nevada and spend the evening with my uncle, my mom's brother and my dear friend, so we could both have a good cry, scream, or just talk, away from the rest of the family. He even paid for the bus package, which included $7 in betting money.

We spent the night talking about Mom and having a great meal. All the pain went away, we both gained closure . . . and that amazing energy came back, about taking charge of my life. "I'm going to get that money I need," I told my uncle. I went out, got $7 in nickels, and hit the slots— something I was new to. I put in four nickels . . . and received $136.

I just stood there . . . and laughed.

I started a company with an idea I had come up with during the darkest years of my depression. Something that allowed me to hang on, and not completely give up on life. WANTED: HERO was born, and it became the very first digital comic book on the Web (and, to my knowledge, still is, at the time of writing this article), offering a handmade comic book in digital format for a single dollar. In February 2005, I had fourteen visitors total. By the end of the first year, I had a total of 750,000 visitors come to *my site. Not bad for something that wasn't supposed to work! Within the first two months, I was making a full-time living, doing what I loved. The future looks so bright and exciting to me . . . and it all started with my depression.*

Go figure.

Mission Impossible

Before depression, your life may have been guided by the search for approval from others—to the point of self-destructiveness, in Jaime's experience.

When you give up the need to display loyalty and seek approval, very often you will find yourself in a place where few have ever gone before. You, like Jaime, will find yourself doing things without the comfort of safety rails ensuring that you are on the right path.

Ironically, the generally accepted signal that you are on the right path—approving nods from those around you—are deceptive and possibly destructive. Depression can heal a life that has been guided in the wrong direction by those accepted signals. In the depths of the pain of depression, you may find that your intended destination no longer seems right—you don't really care about what you or others want you to be. The pain of depression tells you that the only way to go forward is to follow the one idea that keeps you hanging on—because in depression there may be only one thing that gives you hope, and that one thing may seem totally crazy. Depression gives you the clarity of "do or die." Do this one thing, or live in this pain. The pain gives you the power to leave the common path, the predictable life, and the safety rails.

Dream the Impossible Dream

You don't have to go all the way to the bottom of your depression to find the parts of yourself that are lit from within. One way to find the calling within is to explore the following questions.

What is my most grandiose, self-serving fantasy of success or happiness?

What if I believed that the world wants to give me so much more than my most grandiose fantasy?

If you shamelessly indulge in fantasies of love and success, you will find a glimmer of your passion. Set aside your doubts for a moment and believe the following: The question is never "Am I good enough?" Rather, the question is always "Am I generous enough?" The eyes of gentleness see vaunting ambition as unbridled generosity. Just as deeply as you ache for making your dreams come true does the world ache for your gifts. The ache inside of you is meant to drive you toward sharing your gifts with the aching world.

Believe for a moment that the universe is knocking itself out right at this moment to lovingly pour itself out to you. What would you do?

DIRTY LITTLE SECRETS

Why do so many people struggle for so long to realize what they really want to do? Perhaps we should ask instead why some people hide their deepest aspirations like they are dirty little secrets, or hidden perversions. The answer? Because many people grew up with limiting beliefs that told them that success is selfish. If you're struggling with these beliefs, practice saying—and believing—the following affirmations:

"My achievements are my generous gift to the world."

"My desires are links to my most important service to the world."

If you are able to reframe your limiting beliefs in this way, you just might overcome the obstacle of feeling selfish for honoring your ambitions and drive for achievement.

The phrase "service to the world" may sound like dutiful self-sacrifice. In practice, world service is the act of doing that which is most exciting to you. World service is the fulfillment of your vaunting ambitions. It is when you are in alignment with your deepest desires, values, and needs that you are doing what you were meant to do.

Chapter 10

Depression as an Opening to the Mysterious

Depression means that your life needs to change. You may need to prune down the demands you place on yourself or you may need to dare to jump to a bigger playing field in order to make your ambitions happen. But when life changes, you must face the unknown. Albert Einstein said that "the most beautiful thing we can experience is the mysterious. It is the source of all true art and science" (Ulam 1976). As your life is rebuilt and old plans fall away, you will need to gain a sense of the mysterious and an appreciation of the beauty of not knowing or controlling the future.

In her book *When Life Changes or You Wish It Would,* Dr. Carol Adrienne writes, "The question about clarity . . . is really a cry for the security of a guaranteed outcome. 'I won't move until I'm sure I'm going to get what I want.' Waiting for absolute clarity may be a trap that keeps us from acting at all" (2002, p. 203). The ability to step out of the known and rigidly controlled into the expanded boundaries of the mysterious will help you recover from your depression. Research has shown that this capacity to transcend the small self and open to something bigger than the self heals depression (Ellermann and Reed 2001).

The following equations demonstrate how you can create different experiences of the unknown based on your own reactions:

The unknown + trust = excitement, adventure

The unknown + fear and doubt = insecurity, nightmare

If you find yourself facing the unknown with doubt, it is important that you give full expression to your doubt so you can find out what it needs. Your doubt is a part of who you are, and it can be honored without it taking full control of your life.

Each person hears both a voice of doubt and a voice of trust when facing the unknown. Both voices are reasonable and valuable, but they can cause difficulty when they are not balanced. You can discover if one voice is out of balance by writing out a dialogue between the part of you that is hopeful and the part of you that is doubtful, discussing the changes in your life that depression seems to be pointing you toward.

The story of Eleanor, below, illustrates the tug-of-war between these two voices. As you read through her story, pay attention to how her voice of doubt told her she shouldn't bother trying to make new friends, since she was sure to be rejected and she was already in too much pain. Her voice of excitement opened up to the possibility that she could find friends and have fulfilling relationships. Eleanor's story is a successful one: her voice of trust wins out and she creates a rich and rewarding new life for herself.

I was always extremely attached to my mom and never really felt the need for my own friendships because I always had my mom's friendship to fall back on. When my mom passed away, I was left lonely and depressed and had no one to fall back on for any type of emotional support. I never knew how to make lasting friendships while my mom was around because I never felt the need to before. I began seeking out ways that I could possibly make some friends of my own by trying on the new belief that I could have loving, fulfilling friendships other than with my mom, but I was scared to open myself up to possible rejection or getting hurt again, when I was already in emotional pain from my mom's passing. When my family moved, I decided that this was my opportunity to make some friends who didn't know anything about me or how shy I was. I began seeking out clubs I could join. In doing so, I began making friends I had lots in common with and now have many of my own good friends as well as a couple of very close friendships, which I never thought was possible because of my shyness and inexperience.

In Eleanor's story, you see that the depression was related to her need to do something she had never done before—take risks to make new friends. She ventured forth with a new belief: "I can have loving, fulfilling friendships other than with my mom." With this trust she was able to create for herself a network of supportive friends.

EXERCISE: DUKE IT OUT

1. Start with the part of yourself that seems to be dominant in your day-to-day life. If you suffer from depression, most likely your doubting voice is winning the day. In Eleanor's experience, the doubting voice told her to stay in the safety zone so she would not risk rejection.

   It may help to imagine your own doubting voice as a character with a specific look or yourself at a different time in your life. For example, you could imagine the voice of doubt as a nagging mother telling you that you'll just get hurt if you go for what you really want. Or you could imagine the doubter in you as yourself as an awkward teenager at a time when you seemed to lose control over your body and moods. Give this character or part of yourself a chance to say what she or he really wants to say. In your journal, write everything that comes up.

2. Now switch to the other voice, and let your trusting side have full expression. Eleanor's trusting side was evident in her daring to reach out and make new friends. As you did with your voice of doubt, try giving your trusting voice a character or age. You could imagine the voice of trust as a teenager who is daring and bold in challenging convention, if that was your experience. Below are some questions the trusting part of yourself might ask the doubter:

- What do you need?

- How were you deprived?

- How were you cheated?

- What do you want?

- What can I give you?

In your journal, write the doubting voice's answers to these questions.

3. Look at the answers you've come up with. What new belief would empower you to move forward and make the changes in your life that you want to make? For example, Eleanor "began seeking out ways that I could possibly make some friends of my own by trying on the new belief that I could have loving, fulfilling friendships other than with my mom."

The result of this exercise is to achieve complexity, not to banish doubt from your life or proclaim the triumph of hope over all else. Complexity will result in both an honest evaluation of real-world limitations and an openness to the possibilities. Like Eleanor, you can be honest about your personal pain and your limitations and yet move forward to make the changes you need to make.

The integration and balance of trust and doubt create an outlook of not demanding that the world meet your needs but knowing that sometimes miracles happen. You are realistic enough to know that sometimes dreams and relationships end, but you are connected enough to your fierce determination to command your own self-respect. You no longer demand that others show you how worthy you are. You see the balance of your pitfalls and your promise. Most important, you choose. You choose to live a life that focuses on your promise and acknowledges your pitfalls.

Celebrating your mystery means experimenting with life and knowing that there are no mistakes—becoming so strong that you can tolerate your own fragility. Living in the mystery is to stand in the face of your impulses and ask, "Now what?" It means caring too much and caring too little. It is a sad yearning startled by inexplicable joy. It is a crushing tenderness, fragile strangeness, and delicate intricacy. It is the capacity to be astonished at being alive.

You can be both grim and grateful, somehow heavy from your losses but giddy with excitement about the wonders that enter your life. You can be weighed down with the sadness of what will never be, while also feeling reverential about the power of your spirit to explore a bigger world than you ever knew before. These polar-opposite feelings don't cancel each other out; they interact in a complex way to provide nuanced shading to your life.

I DON'T KNOW

To cultivate the power of mystery in your life, you can choose "I don't know" as your primary mantra. Whenever you are faced with a question or a problem, let your final answer be "I don't know" and see what emerges for you. Many times the furious need to find answers, facts, and information can be a desperate attempt to fight the underlying feelings.

When Sam's father was diagnosed with a terminal illness, he spent so much time researching the disease and trying to find alternative cures that he never came to terms with his helplessness and feelings of fear and loss. He couldn't say, I don't know what the cause of this disease is, or how to cure it. He couldn't say, I don't know how to let go of you. He couldn't say, I don't know how to live without you. He couldn't say, I don't know who I am without you.

Instead of opening to his unknowing, he warded off his feelings by urging his father to try various alternative treatments. Rather than tolerating his helplessness, Sam spent his father's final days trying to control his father. He missed out on the opportunity to share his fragility with his father and to hear his father's own terrible grief and vulnerability. He created a combative environment in the hospital on his father's final days. Had he been able to recognize his helplessness, he could have created a softer, more caring environment as they shared these final moments. If he had recognized the harsh reality that he was losing his father, he could have taken care to make these last moments ones of intense intimacy.

FROM RESIGNATION TO REALIGNMENT

Even more difficult than "I don't know" is "No." This morning, my guru presented me with a perplexing koan. My two-year-old son said to me, "How do I get the trolley through the tunnel?" He was trying to get his souvenir trolley, bought recently at a gift shop, through the tunnel on his train track, which was designed for a specific brand of toy trains.

The trolley was much larger than the commercial trains designed for this track. The logical answer was "You can't." It was not the answer he wanted to hear. And so it is with many of your life struggles. While it is important to maintain hope, it is essential not to waste your life trying to defy the laws of human nature. You may ask yourself, "How can I stay in this abusive relationship?" The answer is "I can't," even though it is not the answer you want to hear. You may ask, "How can I get my husband to be the person I want him to be?" The answer is "I can't." You may wonder, "How can I make her see how wrong she is?" The answer is "I can't." You may ask, "How can I make everyone in my life happy?" The answer is "I can't." You may ask, "How can I be the perfect mother, wife, daughter, sister, and professional and still stay sane?" The answer is "I can't." You may have to start recognizing the power of "good enough" over perfect; you may have to lower your standards and realize that life is messy.

Once you say "I can't," you are freed to reorganize your goals, your life, and the ways you spend your time, money, and energy. The gift of resignation is that it allows you to move on. Perhaps you will move on to something bigger and better. Perhaps you will move on to something more humble but more rewarding.

REAL REWARDS

I remember the first time I understood what the word "rewarding" really meant. I found myself using it when applying to graduate programs, saying that I wanted a rewarding and fulfilling job at the end of the line. But then I took a job in France, working in a hospital for the severely handicapped.

Most of the individuals I worked with required full care and would spend their entire lives in wheelchairs. All of them spoke only French, a language I didn't speak or understand very well. Somehow, despite the language barrier and my initial fears about being able to help, I connected deeply with those I cared for and felt that every moment was meaningful—and rewarding.

I realized for the first time what that word meant, and knew that I would spend my life doing truly rewarding work: work that is its own reward. Work that I do because it is helpful and because it's needed and because I enjoy it. Work that opens my eyes and makes me see the world in a whole new way and breaks me out of the smallness of day-to-day concerns. This job effected a profound shift in me, away from the typical dreams of many young students wishing for wealth, status, and the limelight. These goals now seemed silly as I experienced firsthand the rewards of working with people who were considered broken and deserving of pity.

I suspected at the time that there was a direct relationship between the "brokenness" of those I tended and their power as a healing force in my own life. Like depression, all forms of brokenness teach us about what is essential. I learned the meaning of life outside the narrow confines of the able bodied—who use their strength and capacities to earn abstract rewards. I also discovered that the best cure for my existential angst was to do work that I felt in the marrow of my bones to be powerfully meaningful.

Many times when we find the honesty to say "I can't," we begin to find our way toward what we can do, and we realign our lives so that our time and energy are spent in ways that are rewarding in this deepest sense of the word.

Sometimes it's hard to know the difference between "I can't" and "I can." I once heard about a truck that had gone into a tunnel and was too high for the height limit. It got stuck. Someone figured out that the way to get the truck out of the tunnel was to deflate the tires and then tow it out. How do you know for sure that the trolley can't get through the tunnel, as my son wondered, or whether there might be another way to get it out?

This is where depression comes in. Many times depression and the feeling of emptiness are important signals telling you to find some other way to devote your life energies. The role of emptiness as a signal pointing us toward what we find truly rewarding, in defiance of what the world tells us, is illustrated in the story of Terri Amos (2004), Miss USA 1982, spiritual coach, and author of *Message Sent: Retrieving the Gift of Love*:

> I am weeping tears of confusion. I have just been named Miss USA of 1982. The audience is whistling and yelling. Their applause thunders through my brain. . . . But I am not finding a whole lot of joy in this moment. Even Bob Barker, the host of the pageant, says, "Terri, show everyone how happy you are." He can see my face. It has a look of dread. . . . The competitive side of me is thrilled to have won. And, yet, there is a lack I can't describe. My confusion surfaces because there is an emptiness inside me. That's because the love has come from the outside, rather than from within me. . . . I spent my whole life seeking others' approval. And to be quite honest, I often got it. I constantly sought out the next achievement that I could hang on my wall or put in my scrap-book. I was the perfect picture of what a young woman should be, at least most of the time. But this was only on the outside. On the inside I was dying from anger and pain. . . . I constantly judged myself, never letting my mind take a rest. I thought I had to be perfect . . . (p. 15)

Terri found that the ultimate reward, which almost every little girl dreams of—being Miss USA—was meaningless to her. Her empti-ness pushed her toward a rewarding career as a spiritual life coach. She realized that all the glory in the world wasn't personally fulfilling to her. As she began her search for self-approval she shared her journey with others in her writing and coaching. Her story is emblematic of the lesson that what your deepest self finds rewarding may fly in the face of what the whole world tells you should be rewarding.

LOST

When you have gotten off of the path you were on—through failure, loss, or depression that made you say "I can't go on"—you will feel lost. You may feel like a child lost in a shopping mall, distressed, over-whelmed, and knowing that your only hope is that someone finds you.

You may focus your energies on the desperate need to be found. "If only someone could find me and show me the way." The message in depression is sometimes a call to be the person who finds you.

When you are lost, you are actually on the path toward opening to the mystery of your life. If you were hiking in the woods and you found you had gone off the trail you had planned to follow, would you really be lost? No. You would just be off the path that you had chosen. You would be somewhere you had not planned on going. But you would still be in the woods and you could still go on hiking. Many times the function of depression is to get you off the path you had mapped out.

Or, in a more dramatic example, what if you went hiking and you broke your leg and had to be airlifted off a mountain to get to a hospital. Would you be lost? Would that be a terrible waste of a hike? In many ways, getting airlifted off of a mountain would be even more of an adventure than hiking in the woods. It wouldn't be a hike, exactly, but it would be interesting and you would learn many things and experience events that were new to you.

Similarly, depression often results when you have gotten off the path you had planned on. Depression can also result after you are taken off your path by forces outside of your control. Part of the gift of depression is to find how the journey away from your planned path has taken you into a mystery—a path that is deeply meaningful though not what you expected.

In an extreme example from my life, I once planned a day of boating with some friends. But what had been intended to be a recreational activity turned into the most terrifying moment of my life. With no warning, the boat exploded into flames. I vividly remember not knowing whether I would live, feeling my legs burning and not knowing if I still had legs, and not knowing whether my friends had survived. Fortunately, all of us did survive, with only minor injuries and burns.

Of course, I would never have asked for that experience or planned for it in any way. But that moment informed the rest of my life. I knew from that moment that I couldn't live my life with the expectation that it would go on forever. I realized that I could not spend any part of my life "settling" for a person, a place, or a profession that was anything less than what I wanted. That experience allowed me to have empathy for others who had survived terrifying experiences. That empathy ended up being a central part of my profession as a psychotherapist.

It may take many years for you to find meaning in your detours away from your life's predicted path. You may never gain clarity, and it may always remain a mystery. But as my near-death experience shows, even a tragic, terrifying deviation from your plans can take you to places or change your life in ways you never could have imagined. In those moments of feeling dazed and confused, I was certainly lost—in that my actual experience was so different from the events I had planned for that day. Yet those moments became pivotal in informing my life and path toward a healing profession. Even when you feel lost, you may actually be reorienting toward a new direction.

PEOPLE ARE STRANGE

Depression makes you different, strange. If you listen to depression and follow its guidance, people may no longer understand you. The psychologist Carl Jung (1980) wrote that the fundamental task of the human is to individuate, which means to become yourself, even if this means being eccentric or strange. Depression is a force for individuation. Either you become yourself or you stay depressed, it warns.

When you become yourself you become a mystery to others, and even to yourself. You become something you need to explore, to investigate more deeply. When you are no longer rigidly directing the course of your life, you become open to a great curiosity about where you are going. You realize that both you and your life path are a mystery, even to yourself, and you may find that you now have a great need to discover who you really are. What do you really love? What do you really want to do? What do you really think? What do you really feel? Hopefully you will find that you are much stranger than you thought you were. You will most likely find parts of yourself that have long been suppressed because they didn't fit in with your rigid ideas of who you are.

In my work as a psychotherapist, I have come to think that the fundamental nature of the human psyche is contradiction. We are complex and contradictory creatures. I remember once seeing a "surfer dude" on a bus, knitting. Another time, I saw a meek-looking, little old lady stopping traffic, walking across a busy street without even looking.

She appeared to be in full possession of her wits, but her actions seemed recklessly defiant, which posed an interesting contrast to her appearance. In my work, I have observed that people who suffer from harsh depressions may have, buried underneath their pain, a great capacity for happiness. All of us have these strange contradictions within us. Depression is often a call to honor our contradictions, and our strangeness.

Unruly Emotions

To uncover your own strangeness you have to connect more deeply with your unruly emotions, even those that seem unrelated to the person you want to be. It may help you to begin thinking of your own experiences in the way that a great wine connoisseur might approach a venerable bottle of wine. If you were trying to get the full sense of the taste of the wine you would pour yourself a glass and go through the four s's: see, smell, swirl, and sip. Next time you feel out of sorts or encounter a feeling that is intense or unfamiliar, try the four s's:

1. See: Try to get a visual picture of your feeling. If you are mad, is it like a hot fire or an icy-cold, immovable iceberg? Put a picture to your feeling.

2. Smell: As you are experiencing the intense or unfamiliar feeling, take a deep breath in through your nose as if you were smelling. This action will allow you to get closer to the experience and dwell on it rather than pushing it away. For example, if you are feeling angry, you may be tempted to clench up against the feeling in an effort to make it go away, which usually makes your breathing shallower. By breathing in you will connect more deeply with the feeling.

3. Swirl: You will want to mix it up a little. How does this new quality interact with the rest of you? Maybe your anger is like fiery red pepper mixed into the overall sweetness of your personality. Maybe the harshness of your anger provides just what you needed to change your flavor and turn your back on people and places that drain your energy.

4. Sip: You will want to fully taste the new experience. As you allow yourself to feel the full intensity of your anger, for example, note your reactions to it. Is it bitter, sweet, or sour? You might be surprised that you find yourself more energized after tasting your anger. Perhaps you thought you would be crushed by your sadness, but you find that it actually has a calming effect. Allow yourself to indulge and explore your new emotional experience and your reactions to it.

DEPRESSION AND GREATNESS

Opening to the mysterious in your own life will help you claim authority over your existence. You might wonder if there is a relationship between depression and power or greatness on the historical stage. Thorough investigations have not demonstrated a robust relationship between depression and greatness (see Peter Kramer's review of the contradictory evidence in *Against Depression* [2005]). The question does not really lend itself to scientific analysis or quanitification, because greatness is by definition a rare and improbable event. However, the phrase "tormented genius" does seem to hint that depression goes hand in hand with towering genius. In a recent presidential election, each candidate was weighed by the media for his gravitas—his weightiness, seriousness, and preoccupation with matters of the greatest import. Gravitas is related to depression in that it gives a person the capacity to see with a dark eye, to look harsh realities in the face without wincing.

The label of greatness is usually given to those who have taken on a life-or-death struggle, changed their world in the process, and come through the struggle with dignity. We want our leaders to have the ability to go through the fire and survive. Perhaps this explains our demand for gravitas in our leaders.

The word "gravitas" comes from the same Latin root as that of "grief." We sense a sturdiness, a resilience, in those who have grieved and survived. Those who have learned that you can lose so much and continue to live are those we look up to. When we think of gravitas we might also think of gravity—the force that determines planetary orbits. The more weight a planet has, the stronger is its force to pull other objects into its orbit. So too is the case with personal power and perhaps greatness. The more weight a person has, the more losses she has digested; the more grim realities she has faced and survived, the more wisdom and heft she carries.

Abraham Lincoln, known for his role in ending slavery in the United States, may be the leader who is most emblematic of depression's link to greatness. Lincoln's life, as seen from a historical perspective, illustrates the very idea that depression serves to overthrow the inauthentic life, and we see that his depression influenced his distinctiveness and strength. Author Joshua Wolf Shenk argues in his book *Lincoln's Melancholy: How Depression Challenged a President and Fueled His Greatness* (2005b) that Lincoln's depression was not an impediment to his service but rather directly and causally related to his profound achievements. In the *Atlantic Monthly*, Shenk (2005a) writes:

> With Lincoln we have a man whose depression spurred him, painfully, to examine the core of his soul; whose hard work to stay alive helped him develop crucial skills and capacities, even as his depression lingered hauntingly; and whose inimitable character took great strength from the piercing insights of depression, the creative response to it, and a spirit of humble determination forged over decades of deep suffering and earnest longing. (p. 54)

If you are struggling with depression, you can use Lincoln's journey as a guide for your own. Shenk's book itself might serve as a resource that helps you tolerate all of your miserable feelings, for it depicts Lincoln's inner state in his darkest days. If life feels impossible to you, it can be helpful to have a vivid image of someone who has gone before you and made it through. Lincoln used his intense personal pain as a bridge, allowing him to identify with the pain of others, including the hurting and outrage of those who were enslaved in the United States. Like Lincoln, you have the choice to let your pain isolate you from the human race or become the very bridge you walk on to connect with others.

Lincoln's depression may also have directly influenced his capacity to challenge the status quo that maintained the institution of slavery. His depression may have stopped him in his tracks so he could reflect on what was not working in the country and gather energy for making necessary changes. Like Lincoln, you have the choice to keep going in your current life, or stop and listen to the depression so you can understand what needs to be changed in your life.

Lincoln's life and accomplishments can show you how the loss of interest in everyday life is a gift that can help you recognize the oppression of the current regime. Lincoln's depression was an accurate reflection of the hypocrisy of the nation he led—a nation that touted personal liberty while condoning slavery. Like Lincoln, you can experience depressive realism. You can find the gift in your depression if you ask yourself the following questions:

- What is my depression an accurate reflection of?

- What needs to be overthrown in my own life?

- How can I live my life in greater alignment with my deepest values?

These questions, using Lincoln's life as a model, can help you to use your depression to fuel your own greatness.

Lee, a friend of mine, reclaimed authority over his own life when he realized how the very foundations of his belief system were obscuring his deepest value, his desire to connect with others. Because his religious upbringing had taught him to look for sin and to judge harshly, he found it hard to accept himself and others. Like Lincoln, who in the depths of his depression learned to see clearly the hypocrisy of his times, my friend, in his struggle with depression, saw that he wanted connection more than the certainty of his belief system.

Lee said:

> My depression helped me realize that I held some worldviews that were at best nonsensical and at worst incredibly damaging to how I perceived myself and others. Although this happened much later in my life than I wish it had, I went through years of questioning my religious upbringing and noted how it had damaged me psychologically in more ways than I could count. I went through the difficult but ultimately empowering process of questioning everything I had once held dear and came out on the other side of it much happier, more fulfilled, and more open minded in ways I would never have imagined before. I think I wouldn't have bothered to question myself if not for the ways in which my narrow, rigid mind-set kept setting me up to be depressed and miserable.

Like Lincoln, Lee found that his depression fueled the breakdown of the status quo.

It doesn't matter what the status quo is. What matters is that depression leads to a deep reflection and questioning about whether your life is in alignment with your deepest values, desires, and strengths. The story above showed how Lee challenged his deeply rooted fundamentalist beliefs. Another friend of mine said that his deep depression led him to see that his Buddhist practice and devotion was a defense against his deeper feelings:

> *Depression forces me to strip bare certain factors and facades*
> *of my life; depression cured me of Buddhism in my second year*
> *of college. It started with my being dumped by my first serious*
> *girlfriend. I knew her leaving me should have devastated me*
> *emotionally and that I should have had a time of sadness and*
> *healing. All the movies and books I read said I should be sad*
> *and all the people I'd seen get dumped acted hurt. This made*
> *my logical side feel that something was wrong with me. This*
> *crack was the impetus my emotional side was waiting for.*
> *I believe my subconscious created a depression that was begging*
> *me to reevaluate and tear down those walls. The depression*
> *challenged my ideals, my concepts of what it was to be human,*
> *and made me aware that I was going against my nature.*
>
> *Ironically, it was this utter lack of emotion that catalyzed*
> *my depression. I did not understand why I couldn't be sad or*
> *why I couldn't cry. I felt that I should have these feelings.*
> *Instead I had zero energy, no will for things, food, or life.*
> *So I dropped out of all my classes for the semester and spent*
> *all my time lying on my dorm room floor or walking around the*
> *dangerous, snowy city streets, barefoot and unkempt, pondering*
> *it all the while.*
>
> *I had been a practicing Buddhist at the time of my*
> *breakup and depression. One of the end goals of Buddhism*
> *was to follow the middle path, avoiding all extremes. No one*
> *ever warned me to avoid extremely following the middle path.*
> *So, I had to wonder if the emotionless husk I had become was*
> *success! If so, it surely wasn't what I expected. Of course, this*
> *was not the root of my problem, but asking these sorts of*
> *questions of myself helped give me direction. I knew it had*
> *to do with how I was processing my emotions.*

*I left the depression embracing my emotional connections
to the world. I also went from being geared toward thinking that
life was about learning as much as possible to thinking
that life was about experiencing as much as possible. Via the
depression I realized that the Buddhism I had been practicing
was not a quest for enlightenment or self-betterment, but a quest
for external reinforcement to my misbegotten patterns
and contrived needs.*

Here, again, we see how depression opens a person up to the conflict between who he is and how he is living his life. In all three of the stories we've seen—those of Lincoln, Lee, and the Buddhist—we see people who recognized the tension and chose to dismantle the fundamental structures that maintained the status quo. If this is the power of depression, you can see how it can be related to greatness in a prominent leader.

Lincoln changed a nation and brought it into line with its deepest values. Both of my friends directly faced the knowledge that their secure foundations were barriers to what they wanted: connection to others and to their emotional lives. These are the makings of personal power and greatness: the courage to change foundational beliefs rather than look the other way, to acknowledge the inner rumblings telling you that there is more to who you are than what you currently know.

In this way, depression connected all of these people to their own mystery. My friends didn't leave their foundational belief systems to embrace yet another. They leapt and created a life that was unique to them. They went out into a world they didn't fully understand, having thrown out the maps they had inherited. Their depression forced them to move beyond their lives of quiet desperation, into a life that was more uncertain, more unknown, with less control but with a sense of aliveness and the mystery of unfolding their selves.

These stories support a relationship between depression and creativity. If depression tears down existing structures, then the person is left to create a new structure in a new life. Author Roger Housden, in his review of Rembrandt's life, wrote that since ancient times it was believed that

anyone eminent in philosophy, poetry, or the arts was likely to be melancholic. It was both feared as the cause of madness and envied as the source of genius. During the Renaissance, it was considered indispensable for creativity of any kind. . . . Depression, which takes you down into yourself, may be the fastest means of access to your own true needs. It can certainly be the catalyst for creative endeavor. (2005a, pp. 24–25)

Depression may be associated with greatness because it is a force for becoming the author of your own life. Most of us make many of our major life choices for all the wrong reasons. We cannot help but be shaped by the wants and expectations of our families, friends, and subcultures. Depression is a call to find your own weight, to give yourself permission to become a leader, to create your own worldview. The pain of depression is caused by the sense of helplessness associated with unmooring yourself from what is familiar and has guided your life for many years. The gift of depression is that you reclaim your capacity to create your own rules.

Of course, most people who are depressed don't go on to have earth-shattering greatness. Many people who struggle with depression are shattered by the experience. But greatness is the capacity to have your foundations shaken or shattered and to find the strength to rebuild your identity based on the most authentic materials you can find within yourself. In this way, depression allows you to access your inner greatness: the capacity to overcome and to move forward with a sober view of your limitations and possibilities. Your greatness may not be recognized on the historical stage, but you can become a hero to yourself. This is the ultimate lesson of depression: you don't need a hero out there to save you, you don't need a following out in the world to recognize your greatness. You become your own hero, who has the power to give yourself what you need.

This ability to take care of yourself will give you an inner feeling of greatness. Feeling great often means feeling a sense of the sacred in ordinary life, and no small part of the sacred is that which is mysterious. For this reason, the unknowable and unsolvable problem of depression can become a blessing: unsolvable problems bring you into contact with the sacred. When you come to your wit's end, you open to the possibility of a world out there that is larger than you. Ultimately, this is the cure and cause of depression—to push you out of your small world and open you to possibilities and deeper explorations.

If the only thing you gain from your depression is a sense of humility at not being able to understand it, then that is no small thing. Humility can be a sweet liberation. Humility can free you from needing to know, from needing to be right, from needing to prove yourself, from needing to chastise yourself. If you can embrace the sense of relief that comes with being released from these unrelenting demands, then you will have found the gift of depression.

Chapter 11

In Defense of Defensiveness

In the movie *Sideways*, the main character treasures a very special bottle of wine that he has saved for a special occasion. The woman he falls in love with tells him that with a bottle of wine like that you don't need a special occasion to drink it. In one of the final scenes, we see him, on a regular day—in fact, a bad day—drinking this highly treasured wine out of a plastic cup, in a diner.

This scene offers a wonderful picture of what you need to do for yourself in the depths of depression. Give yourself whatever you need now. Don't save your treasures for some later date. The deeper the depression, the more you need to pull out all of the stops.

This advice differs from what I've said in the rest of this book. Before, I have told you that you need to listen to your pain and hear what it has to say about healing your life, rather than indulging in comforting behaviors that obscure its message. In this chapter, however, I am saying that there are situations in which you should defend against the pain—just making it go away so that you can begin to listen to it.

WHEN DEPRESSION IS NOT A GIFT

In severe depression, there is a serious risk with suicidal thoughts and actions: up to 15 percent of those with severe major depressive disorder will die by suicide. It is therefore imperative that you seek immediate relief from the pain you are feeling. Some conditions that indicate that you should get rid of the pain before proceeding are the following:

- Suicidal crisis

- Severe depression

- Unmet basic needs, such as in poverty

- Current physical or emotional abuse

- Societal discrimination

- Alcohol and drug abuse

- Extreme stressors

- Trauma

As I stated above, if you are experiencing severe depression and suicidal thoughts, you should aggressively treat your symptoms of depression. This may mean seeking hospitalization and being evaluated for the need for antidepressant medications. Because the risks of suicide are real in the case of severe depression, you will need as much support as you can get from friends, family, mental health care providers, and any other resources you can find. If you are worried about your safety, below are some actions you can take immediately to protect yourself:

- Seek social support.

- Remove any lethal means (such as guns, medications, knives).

- Remove any reminders of suicidal models (such as music by goth bands).

- Remove yourself from ongoing stressors.

- Engage in activities you enjoy or that will distract you.

Medication

Many people who suffer from depression will be prescribed medications as part of their treatment. If you decide that your pain is so great that you need to bolster your resistance to the depression, then you might consider getting evaluated for antidepressant medication treatment. In some cases, people cannot even do the work of exploring the meaning of their depression without some help from these medications. In this way, medication can be a part of your journey to understanding the deeper meaning of your depression. Or, in some cases, the depression may be a side effect of a medication or have another biological cause. Your physician can help you determine if this is the case.

In addition to coping with stressful events, you have the power to make life choices that will change your life so as to relieve stress. Neuroscientist Dr. Mona Lisa Schulz reflects on the effectiveness of antidepressants in her book *The New Feminine Brain: How Women Can Develop Their Inner Strengths, Genius, and Intuition*. She shares her observation that the leading class of antidepressants, SSRIs (selective serotonin reuptake inhibitors), are often effective but that they do not offer a long-term strategy for healing depression. She writes, "If a patient chooses not to engage in therapy, and doesn't change what is aggravating her mood, no SSRI will prevent the depression's return. SSRIs can't Scotch-tape a woman's mood together for long if she is in an abusive relationship and doesn't do a 'relationship-ectomy' or if she's spending forty hours a week in an irritating job that doesn't use her talents and skills" (Schulz 2005, p. 153). Medications can help your short-term recovery from depression, but it is worth it to explore the deeper meanings of your depression, so that you can hear its message to change your life over the long term.

EXERCISE: WHO'S THE BOSS?

You are bigger than your depression. You may be able to learn from your depression, or you may be able to manage your depression, but you are not your depression. It is something that you have, or maybe it is even something that has you. But at the end of the day, you are not your depression. The following exercise will help you to see this truth.

1. Take a piece of paper and crumple it up like a piece of trash. Set the crumpled paper on a table in front of you. Tell yourself that this is your depression. Take a deep breath and see what it feels like to have your depression outside of yourself for a moment.

2. Look at the crumpled piece of paper and ask it, "Who are you?" In your journal, write down any answers that come up. Pay particular attention if someone else's name comes up in your responses.

3. If someone else's name does come up, ask yourself if you are depressed about someone else's life, or if you are depressed for someone else. Children will often take on a parent's depression. Sometimes if someone you love is depressed, you will feel depressed as a way of feeling close to them. If someone you loved was depressed when he or she died, you may feel that being depressed is a way to feel like that person is still present. Explore the possibility that your depression is not yours but somebody else's. If you have determined that the depression is yours, move on to the next steps. If the depression is someone else's, write a list of things you can do to feel connected to that person that don't involve being depressed. Do those things.

4. Once again, look at the crumpled piece of paper representing your depression and ask it the following questions:

   ■ "What do you want me to do?"

   ■ "Who do you want me to be?"

   ■ "What do you want me to know?"

5. Ignore any answers that are negative and keep going until something useful comes up. Write down everything that seems helpful. Reflect on these answers.

6. Write down a list of ways that you can do, be, or know the things that are on your list. For example, if your depression wants you to take a break from too many demands, make a plan to give yourself the break you need.

7. Now, take the crumpled piece of paper and throw it in a garbage can.

8. Finally, write a letter to your depression. Tell the depression that you are grateful for the many lessons that it has brought you. Write down the gifts of your depression. Tell your depression that you want to get your lessons in another way from now on. Promise yourself that you are willing to listen carefully and pay attention to your life without depression.

Chapter 12

Final Thoughts

Now that you have reached the end of this book, you have journeyed through your depression and out into a brighter light. I hope you have found a deeper meaning in your depression. If what this book says is true—if you have listened to the pain of your depression—your life will be different now.

Give yourself full permission to experience your new life without depression. Change is uncomfortable, and that discomfort is part of the human condition. If you were depressed for a long time, it may feel strange to now be without your depression. Just remind yourself that change is uncomfortable—even positive change. Tell yourself you are willing to feel unsettled for a short while in exchange for a life without depression.

You may also have to give yourself permission to live a happy life when others around you are still depressed. Once, I gave a workshop on the gifts depression has to offer, and two beautiful young women, who were poised to set the world on fire, told me about the depths of their depression, saying that everyone they knew was also depressed. I have heard from clients who live in the wealthiest areas that half of their neighbors are taking antidepressants. I began to wonder whether in certain circles being depressed has become an epidemic, or, dare I say it, a trend.

Whether or not these reports are exaggerations, it is true that you may be surrounded by people who are still depressed, even though you have recovered. Misery loves company, as they say. If you are in this situation, do not let yourself be pulled down by the others around you. You may fear that the new happy you will not be accepted by others who knew you when you were depressed. One way to handle this situation is to give yourself permission to set a new standard. Let yourself be the role model of happiness in your circle of friends or family. Think of someone you know who has been an inspiration to you. If you have succeeded in healing your life, let yourself become the inspiration for others.

NOW WHAT?

As you move into your new life, you may wonder how you will prevent yourself from falling into a depression again. The answer is to continue to listen to your pain. But from now on don't wait for your pain to get so big that it cripples you. You can prevent a depression by listening to the whispers that you hear and not waiting for the messages to become loud, booming shouts.

The best way to move through your pain, despair, sadness, loneliness, fatigue, emptiness, and other symptoms of depression is not to be afraid of them. When these feelings come up, don't push them aside. If you listen to the pain when it first comes up, you can move through it very quickly. If you are tired, listen to your body. What do you need? Do something to meet that need, even if only in some small way. If you begin to feel a twinge of worthlessness, begin to look at ways you are spending your time that may not be worthwhile.

It is a balancing act—to let yourself be happy without being afraid of the pain. It requires that you trust that the pain has a message and that you need only to listen to it and settle back into your happiness. The pain is trying to redirect you toward a course that will lead you toward your happiness. The pain is meant to heal you.

Support Group

One thing you can do to maintain your happiness is to form a study group centered on this book. Find a few friends or family members and ask them to read the book and meet regularly to discuss it. This will accomplish two things. First, you will bring your struggle out of the darkness if you have felt alone in your depression. Second, you can support each other in your efforts to keep the focus positive and find the gifts of your depression. Listening to your pain while accepting your happiness is not an easy path to stay on, and the people in your support group can help you by providing feedback if you go too far in one direction or another. Others can point out if you are not listening to your pain, or if you are not giving yourself full permission to experience the happiness of healing your life.

THE END OF DEPRESSION

The end of your depression is the beginning of a new life for you. Begin to expect big surprises, big disruptions, dreams coming true, and the graceful departure of outworn dreams. It is time for you to explode onto the scene of your own life. This means that you will become fascinated with your own inner workings.

An ancient philosopher said, "Be kind, for everyone you meet is engaged in a great struggle." That means you, too. What is your great struggle? Can you be your own cheerleader? Your own coach? Can you pat yourself on the back and say, "Good game," whether you win or lose? Can you make yourself right instead of wrong? The end of depression comes when you can see the great struggle you have been through, see how valiant you have been, and be kind to yourself.

References

Adrienne, C. 2002. *When Life Changes or You Wish It Would: How to Survive and Thrive in Uncertain Times.* New York: Morrow.

Affleck, G., H. Tennen, S. Croog, and S. Levine. 1987. Causal attribution, perceived benefits, and morbidity after a heart attack: An eight-year study. *Journal of Consulting and Clinical Psychology* 55:29–35.

Alloy, L. B., and L. Abrahamson. 1998. Depressive realism: Four theoretical perspectives. In *Cognitive Processes in Depression,* edited by L. Alloy. New York: Guilford Press.

American Psychiatric Association. 2000. *Diagnostic and Statistical Manual of Mental Disorders.* 4th ed., Text revision. Washington, DC: Author.

Amos, T. 2004. *Message Sent: Retrieving the Gift of Love.* Redondo Beach, CA: WorldofLite Publishing.

Bach, R. 1989. *Illusions: The Adventures of a Reluctant Messiah.* New York: Dell.

Buckingham, M., and D. O. Clifton. 2001. *Now, Discover Your Strengths*. New York: Free Press.

Burns, D. 1980. *Feeling Good: The New Mood Therapy*. New York: Avon Books.

Caddy, E., and D. E. Platts. 1992. *Bringing More Love into Your Life: The Choice Is Yours*. Scotland: Findhorn Press.

Caplan, S., and G. Lang. 1995. *Grief's Courageous Journey*. Oakland, CA: New Harbinger Publications.

Childre, D., and H. Martin. 1999. *The HeartMath Solution*. San Francisco: HarperCollins.

Childre, D., and D. Rozman. 2003. *Transforming Anger: The HeartMath Solution for Letting Go of Rage, Frustration, and Irritation*. Oakland, CA: New Harbinger Publications.

Chou, K., and I. Chi. 2001. Stressful life events and depressive symptoms: Social support and sense of control as mediators or moderators? *International Journal of Aging and Human Development* 52:155–71.

Clark, R. C. 2002. Effects of individual and family hardiness on caregiver depression and fatigue. *Research in Nursing and Health* 25:37–48.

Collins, K. A., H. A. Westra, D. J. A. Dozois, and D. D. Burns. 2004. Gaps in accessing treatment for anxiety and depression: Challenges for the delivery of care. *Clinical Psychology Review* 24:583–616.

Coyne, J. C., C. M. Pepper, and H. Flynn. 1999. Significance of prior episodes of depression in two patient populations. *Journal of Consulting and Clinical Psychology* 67:76–81.

Das, L. S. 2003. *Letting Go of the Person You Used to Be*. New York: Broadway Books.

Dobbs, D. 2005. Antidepressants: Good drugs or good marketing? *Scientific American Mind* 1:10–13.

Einstein, A. 1976. Quoted in Ulam, S. M., *Adventures of a Mathematician*. New York: Scribner's Sons.

Ellermann, C. R., and P. G. Reed. 2001. Self-transcendence and depression in middle-age adults. *Western Journal of Nursing Research* 23:698–713.

Ellis, A. 2001. *Overcoming Destructive Beliefs, Feelings, and Behaviors: New Directions for Rational Emotive Behavior Therapy.* New York: Prometheus Books.

Gafni, M. 2001. *Soul Prints: Your Path to Fulfillment.* New York: Fireside.

Gelso, C. J., and S. Woodhouse. 2003. Toward a positive psychotherapy: Focus on human strength. In *Counseling Psychology and Optimal Human Functioning,* edited by B. Walsh. Mahwah, NJ: Erlbaum.

Glassman, A. H., J. E. Helzer, L. S. Covey, L. B. Cottler, F. Stetner, J. E. Tipp, and J. Johnson. 1990. Smoking, smoking cessation and major depression. *Journal of the American Medical Association* 264:1546–49.

Gut, E. 1989. *Productive and Unproductive Depression.* New York: Basic Books.

Henriques, G. 2000. Depression: Disease or behavioral shutdown mechanism? *Journal of Science and Health Policy* 1:204–24.

Hillman, J. 1983. *Healing Fictions.* Dallas: Spring.

Hirschfeld, R. M., M. B. Keller, S. Panico, B. S. Arons, D. Barlow, F. Davidoff, J. Endicott, J. Froom, M. Goldstein, J. M. Gorman, R. G. Marek, T. A. Maurer, R. Meyer, K. Phillips, J. Ross, T. L. Schwenk, S. S. Sharfstein, M. E. Thase, and R. J. Wyatt. 1997. The National Depressive and Manic-Depressive Association Consensus Statement on the undertreatment of depression. *Journal of the American Medical Association* 277:333–40.

Holden, C. 2003. Future brightening for depression treatments. *Science* 302:810-13.

Honos-Webb, L. 2005a. *The Gift of ADHD: How to Transform Your Child's Problems into Strengths.* Oakland, CA: New Harbinger Publications.

———. 2005b. The meaning vs. the medical model in the empirically supported treatment program: A consideration of the empirical evidence. *Journal of Contemporary Psychotherapy* 35:55–65.

Honos-Webb, L., L. Gal, A. Shaikh, E. A. Harrick, J. A. Lani, L. M. Knobloch, M. Surko, and W. Stiles. 2002. Rewards and risks of exploring negative emotion: An assimilation model account. In *The Verbal Communication of Emotions: Interdisciplinary Approaches,* edited by S. Fussell. Hillsdale, NJ: Erlbaum.

Honos-Webb, L., and L. M. Leitner. 2001. How using the DSM causes damage: A client's report. *Journal of Humanistic Psychology* 41:36–56.

———. 2002. Therapy case formulation as interventional assessment. *Humanistic Psychologist* 30:102–13.

Honos-Webb, L., W. Stiles, and L. S. Greenberg. 2003. A method of rating assimilation in psychotherapy based on markers of change. *Journal of Counseling Psychology* 50:189–98.

Honos-Webb, L., W. Stiles, L. S. Greenberg, and R. Goldman. 1998. Assimilation analysis of process-experiential psychotherapy: A comparison of two cases. *Psychotherapy Research* 8:264–86.

———. 2006. Responsibility for "being there": An assimilation analysis. In *Qualitative Research Methods for Psychologists: Introduction to Empirical Studies,* edited by C. T. Fischer. New York: Elsevier.

———. 2004. The healing power of telling stories in psychotherapy. In *Studies in Meaning 2,* edited by J. D. Raskin and S. K. Bridges. New York: Pace University Press.

Honos-Webb, L., M. Surko, W. Stiles, and L. S. Greenberg. 1999. Assimilation of voices in psychotherapy: The case of Jan. *Journal of Counseling Psychology* 46:448–60.

Housden, R. 2005a. *How Rembrandt Reveals Your Beautiful, Imperfect Self: Life Lessons from the Master.* New York: Harmony Books.

———. 2005b. *Seven Sins for a Life Worth Living.* New York: Harmony Books.

Isaacowitz, D. M., G. E. Vaillant, and M. Seligman. 2003. Strengths and satisfaction across the adult lifespan. *International Journal of Aging and Human Development* 57:181–201.

Jacobson, N. S., and S. D. Hollon. 1996. Cognitive-behavior therapy versus pharmacotherapy: Now that the jury's returned its verdict, it's time to present the rest of the evidence. *Journal of Consulting and Clinical Psychology* 64:74–80.

Joiner, T. E., G. I. Metalsky, F. Gencoz, and T. Gencoz. 2001. The relative specificity of excessive reassurance-seeking to depressive symptoms and diagnoses among clinical samples of adults and youth. *Journal of Psychopathology and Behavioral Assessment* 23:35–41.

Jung, C. G. 1980. *The Archetypes and the Collective Unconscious.* Princeton, NJ: Princeton University Press.

———. 2001. Quoted in Buckingham, M., and D. O. Clifton, *Now, Discover Your Strengths.* New York: Free Press.

Khema, A. 2001. *Being Nobody, Going Nowhere: Meditations on the Buddhist Path.* Sommerville, MA: Wisdom Publications.

Kierkegaard, S. 1992. Quoted in Caddy, E., and D. E. Platts, *Bringing More Love into Your Life: The Choice Is Yours.* Scotland: Findhorn Press.

Kirshenbaum, M. 2004. *Everything Happens for a Reason.* New York: Harmony Books.

Kramer, P. 2005. *Against Depression.* New York: Viking.

Kumar, S. M. 2005. *Grieving Mindfully.* Oakland, CA: New Harbinger Publications.

Lappé, F. M., and J. Perkins. 2004. *You Have the Power: Choosing Courage in a Culture of Fear.* New York: Tarcher.

Leitner, L. M., A. J. Faidley, and M. A. Celentana. 2000. Diagnosing human meaning making: An experiential constructivist approach. In *Constructions of Disorder: Meaning-Making Frameworks for Psychotherapy,* edited by R. A. Neimeyer and J. D. Raskin. Washington, DC: American Psychological Association.

Lerner, D., D. A. Adler, H. Chang, L. Lapitsky, M. Y. Hood, C. Perissinotto, J. Reed, T. J. McLaughlin, E. R. Berndt, and W. H. Rogers. 2004. Unemployment, job retention and productivity loss among employees with depression. *Psychiatric Services* 55:1371–78.

Leuchter, A. F., I. A. Cook, E. A. Witte, M. Morgan, and M. Abrams. 2002. Changes in brain function of depressed subjects during treatment with placebo. *American Journal of Psychiatry* 159:122–29.

Levinson, D. 2004. *Surviving the Death of Your Spouse.* Oakland, CA: New Harbinger Publications.

Lewinsohn, P. M., P. Rohde, J. R. Seeley, and S. A. Fischer. 1993. Age-cohort changes in the lifetime occurrence of depression and other mental disorders. *Journal of Abnormal Psychology* 102:110–20.

Lin, E. H., and C. Peterson. 1990. Pessimistic explanatory style and response to illness. *Behavioral Research and Therapy* 28:243–48.

Marra, T. 2005. *Dialectical Behavior Therapy in Private Practice: A Practical and Comprehensive Guide.* Oakland, CA: New Harbinger Publications.

Mohr, D. C., S. L. Hart, L. Julain, C. Catledge, L. Honos-Webb, L. Vella, and E. T. Tasch. 2005. Telephone administered psychotherapy for depression. *Archives of General Psychiatry* 62:1007–14.

Moore, T. 1992. *Care of the Soul.* New York: HarperPerennial.

Naparstek, B. 1997. *Your Sixth Sense.* San Francisco: HarperCollins.

Park, N., C. Peterson, and M. Seligman. 2004. Strengths of character and well-being. *Journal of Social and Clinical Psychology* 23:603–19.

Peterson, C., M. Seligman, and G. E. Vaillant. 1988. Pessimistic explanatory style is a risk factor for physical illness: A thirty-five-year longitudinal study. *Journal of Personality and Social Psychology* 55:23–27.

Potter-Efron, P. S., and R. T. Potter-Efron. 1999. *The Secret Message of Shame: Pathways to Hope and Healing.* Oakland, CA: New Harbinger Publications.

Prather, H. 1983. *Notes to Myself.* New York: Bantam.

Rosen, D. 2002. *Transforming Depression.* York Beach, ME: Nicolas-Hays.

Schulz, M. L. 2005. *The New Feminine Brain: How Women Can Develop Their Inner Strengths, Genius, and Intuition.* New York: Free Press.

Schulz, M. S., P. A. Cowan, C. P. Cowan, and R. T. Brennan. 2004. Coming home upset: Gender, marital satisfaction and the daily spillover of workday experience into marriage. *Journal of Family Psychology* 18:250–63.

Shenk, J. W. 2005a. Lincoln's great depression. *Atlantic Monthly*, October, 52–68.

———. 2005b. *Lincoln's Melancholy: How Depression Challenged a President and Fueled His Greatness*. Boston: Houghton Mifflin.

Taylor, S. E., M. E. Kemeny, G. M. Reed, J. E. Bower, and T. L. Gruenewald. 2000. Psychological resources, positive illusions and health. *American Psychologist* 55:99–109.

Tedeschi, R. G., C. L. Park, and L. G. Calhoun, eds. 1998. *Posttraumatic Growth: Positive Changes in the Aftermath of Crisis*. Mahwah, NJ: Erlbaum.

Tennen, H., and G. Affleck. 2002. Benefit-finding and benefit-reminding. In *Handbook of Positive Psychology*, edited by C. R. Snyder and S. J. Lopez. Oxford: Oxford University Press.

Ulam, S. M. 1976. *Adventures of a Mathematician*. New York: Scribner's Sons.

Whybrow, P. C. 2005. *American Mania: When More Is Not Enough*. New York: Norton.

Williamson, M. 2005. *The Gift of Change*. San Francisco: HarperSanFrancisco.

Wingert, P., and B. Kantrowitz. 2002. Young and depressed. *Newsweek*, October 7, 52–60.

Yalom, I. D. 2002. *The Gift of Therapy: An Open Letter to a New Generation of Therapists and Their Patients*. New York: HarperCollins.

Lara Honos-Webb, Ph.D., is a licensed clinical psychologist in private practice in Walnut Creek, CA. She is author of *The Gift of ADHD* and more than twenty-five scholarly articles. Her work has been featured in *Newsweek*, *The Wall Street Journal*, and *Publisher's Weekly*, as well as newspapers across the country and national radio and television programs. She specializes in the treatment of ADHD, depression, and the psychology of pregnancy and motherhood and speaks regularly on her areas of expertise. Honos-Webb completed a two-year postdoctoral research fellowship at University of California, San Francisco, and has been an assistant professor teaching graduate students. She offers telephone therapy to residents anywhere in California. Visit her Web site at **www.visionarysoul.com.**

Some Other
New Harbinger Titles

Freeing the Angry Mind, Item 4380 $14.95

Living Beyond Your Pain, Item 4097 $19.95

Transforming Anxiety, Item 4445 $12.95

Integrative Treatment for Borderline Personality Disorder, Item 4461 $24.95

Depressed and Anxious, Item 3635 $19.95

Is He Depressed or What?, Item 4240 $15.95

Cognitive Therapy for Obsessive-Compulsive Disorder, Item 4291 $39.95

Child and Adolescent Psychopharmacology Made Simple, Item 4356 $14.95

ACT* on Life Not on Anger, Item 4402 $14.95

Overcoming Medical Phobias, Item 3872 $14.95

Acceptance & Commitment Therapy for Anxiety Disorders, Item 4275 $58.95

The OCD Workbook, Item 4224 $19.95

Neural Path Therapy, Item 4267 $14.95

Overcoming Obsessive Thoughts, Item 3813 $14.95

The Interpersonal Solution to Depression, Item 4186 $19.95

Get Out of Your Mind & Into Your Life, Item 4259 $19.95

Dialectical Behavior Therapy in Private Practice, Item 4208 $54.95

The Anxiety & Phobia Workbook, 4th edition, Item 4135 $19.95

Loving Someone with OCD, Item 3295 $15.95

Overcoming Animal & Insect Phobias, Item 3880 $12.95

Overcoming Compulsive Washing, Item 4054 $14.95

Angry All the Time, Item 3929 $13.95

Handbook of Clinical Psychopharmacology for Therapists, 4th edition, Item 3996 $55.95

Writing For Emotional Balance, Item 3821 $14.95

Surviving Your Borderline Parent, Item 3287 $14.95

When Anger Hurts, 2nd edition, Item 3449 $16.95

Calming Your Anxious Mind, Item 3384 $12.95

Ending the Depression Cycle, Item 3333 $17.95

Call **toll free, 1-800-748-6273,** or log on to our online bookstore at **www.newharbinger.com** to order. Have your Visa or Mastercard number ready. Or send a check for the titles you want to New Harbinger Publications, Inc., 5674 Shattuck Ave., Oakland, CA 94609. Include $4.50 for the first book and 75¢ for each additional book, to cover shipping and handling. (California residents please include appropriate sales tax.) Allow two to five weeks for delivery.

Prices subject to change without notice.